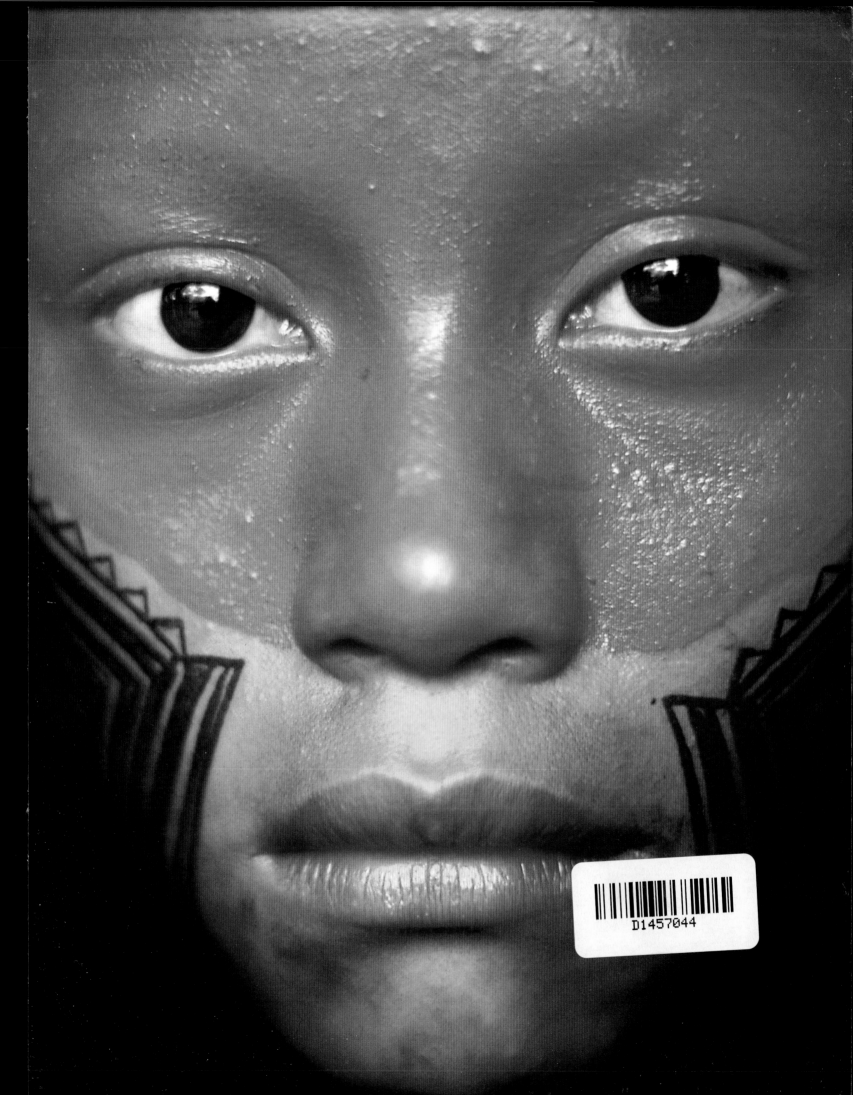

To the Mekranoti,
wishing them strength
in their attempt
to remain Mekranoti

Gustaaf Verswijver

Mekranoti

Living among the Painted People of the Amazon

Prestel   Munich · New York

Contents

Introduction

As an aspiring anthropologist in the 1970s, I hoped to do fieldwork among the Pende of southwestern Zaire. In Africa, of course, just as any Belgian anthropologist would do. Colleagues advised me not to go to Zaire, however, and so I decided to study one of the pastoral groups occupying the lower Omo River in southwestern Ethiopia. Due to the shaky political situation there, that plan also fell through. Having failed twice, I decided to abandon my African aspirations and to focus instead on an Indian group in what seemed to me at the time to be the most mysterious place in the world: the Amazon basin. The Kaiapo Indians of central Brazil intrigued me, not only because research on material culture—my initial research topic—seemed to promise rich results but also because photographs of the Indians simply fascinated me. I was a bit hesitant, because no recent reliable data was available, so it was impossible to conjecture much about them. Nonetheless, I decided to work among the Mekranoti, in the early 1970s the most isolated group among the Kaiapo.

The Kaiapo speak a dialect belonging to the Gê group of languages and so are linguistically related to the Boróro, the Indians made famous through Claude Lévi-Strauss's gripping descriptions in his celebrated book *Tristes Tropiques* (1955). Kaiapo territory extends from the southeast portion of the State of Pará to the extreme northeast of Mato Grosso. The villages are dispersed along the upper course of the Iriri, Bacajá, Fresco, and other tributaries of the powerful Xingú River, occupying

Kaiapo isn't a name the Indians gave themselves, but is a term neighboring Indians use to refer to them. In all likelihood, it means "resembling apes" and probably has to do with a ritual during which Kaiapo men perform short daily dances wearing monkey masks.

a territory the size of Austria. This territory is covered almost entirely by tropical rain forest, with a few open grasslands in the eastern part. Mekranoti territory occupies a plateau some three to four hundred meters above sea level. Small, often isolated hillocks about three hundred meters in height at the most are scattered about. The major rivers are fed by countless creeks and brooks often too small to have been named by the Brazilians. Recent estimates put the total Kaiapo population at about 3,500, a figure that places them among the 15 most important groups of Indians in Amazonia.

Kaiapo villages are relatively big by Amazonian standards. The average one has a population of between two and five hundred people. In 1974, when I first arrived in Mekranoti (the name of the village is the same as that of the group), it had 250 inhabitants. Today, the Mekranoti population has increased to about six hundred, divided over several villages.

The ancestral Kaiapo inhabited the region along the lower course of the Tocantins River from time immemorial. This area covered open grasslands crossed here and there by rivers flanked by gallery woods. The consequences of the first direct contacts between the Kaiapo and whites were catastrophic, to say the least. At the beginning of the nineteenth century, gangs of colonizers overran Kaiapo villages claiming many victims among the men and children. Many women and children were carried off and sold as slaves in towns and cities to the north. The Kaiapo were virtually helpless against this onslaught. Although more numerous than the colonizers, they fought with clubs against muskets. To save themselves, the Kaiapo left their traditional territory and fled westward into the hinterland, a haven that proved short-lived. The frontiers of colonization were being pushed back unremittingly, and 30 years later the conquerors reappeared. This time, their impending arrival inspired discord among the Kaiapo, some of whom wanted to establish friendly relations with the "tribe of pale foreigners" and have access to their trade goods, especially muskets. The opponents of this idea pointed to the dangers posed by such relations, citing the many Indian deaths from unknown causes that had followed initial contact with whites. Caused by exposure to western diseases, these deaths were believed by the Indians to have been caused by the whites' magical powers. These internal tensions led to a series of divisions, as a result of which the big ancestral group broke up into several sub-groups. Some of these groups, such as the Mekranoti (or better, Mekrãgnoti, "the people with big red paint on their faces"), moved inland and settled in an area covered almost entirely by rain forests.

From the beginning of the twentieth century on, the Mekranoti and other Kaiapo groups started attacking Brazilian settlers who approached their new habitat. Through these raids, the Indians acquired rifles, pots and pans, machetes, clothing, and other trade goods. In the 1950s, government envoys penetrated Kaiapo territory, contacting most of the groups. Contacted peacefully in 1953, the Mekranoti soon fled back into the forest, something they did repeatedly. In 1967, a missionary and his family settled among them, staying for two years. After he left, other missionaries occasionally visited the village, but permanent contact was only established in 1972, when missionaries of the Summer Institute of Linguistics arrived.

I first visited Mekranoti in November 1974. In the seven years that followed, I spent more than thirty-three months there, as well as an additional three months among other, closely related Kaiapo groups. In all, I made ten trips to the villages, each time spending between one and nine months there. After a long absence, I returned for brief annual visits between 1989 and 1992. This book recounts the highlights of my three years among the Mekranoti. The first two chapters are arranged chronologically, while the others are arranged by season, blending events that occurred in different years.

A few caveats are necessary. During some of my stays with the Mekranoti, I was accompanied by individuals sent by the Brazilian government or by Belgian friends or family members. If they aren't mentioned in the following pages, there are two reasons. First of all, it would make for a confusing narrative. Second, the reactions and behavior of some of these short-term visitors wasn't always exemplary, and I don't wish to embarrass them. Finally, out of respect for the anonymity of my Mekranoti friends, I've changed all of the names of people mentioned in the book.

Belém

Amazon River

Santarém

← **Manaus**

Tapayoz River

Penetecáua River

Altamira

Jaraucú

Xingú River

Aráca

Araweté

Assuriní

Bacajá River

Iriri River

Parakaná

Itacaiúnas River

Itaitúba

Jamanxim River

Curuá River

Ipixuna River

Marabá

São Felix do Xingú

Araguaia River

Northern Mekranoti
(Baú village)

Baú River

Xixé River

Kuben-
krankênh

Gorotíre

Carolina

Curuaés (Pitiaá) River

Mekranoti

Curuá River

Mekranoti

MEKRANOTI

Fresco River

Redenção

Conceição
do Araguaia

Cachimbo
(Army Post)

Miracema
do Norte

Peixoto de Azevedo River

Kreen Akróre

Araguacema

Tocantins River

Southern
Mekranoti

← **Alta Floresta**

Tapirapé

Liberdade River

*Bananal
Island*

**Xingú
National
Park**

Karajá

Brasília

Cuiabá

Rio de Janeiro

São Paulo

■ Brazilian agglomerations

▲ Kaiapo villages

▲ Mekranoti village where the author stayed the most.
This village split up in the early 1980s into two
separate communities; the new sites are indicated
with ▲

Area inhabited by the Kaiapo
in the 18th century

Aráca, Araweté, etc.: Other ethnic groups

The following rules apply for the pronunciation of Mekranoti words:

- emphasis is invariably placed on the last syllable;
- hyphenations mark the beginning of a suffix which is not emphasized;
- "u" should be pronounced as the short *ou* in French;
- "à" is like the u in the English word *luck;*
- "y" is like the ü in the German word *über,* but always short and slightly centralized;
- "ê" is like the i in the Dutch word *ik,* always pronounced short;
- "ô" is like the ô in the French word *côte,* with the lips strongly rounded;
- the tilde ~ marks nasalization;
- "ng" is like the ng in the English word *king;*
- "nh" is like the gn in the French word *compagnon;*
- "j" is like the y in the English word *young.*

The Anthropologist Who Came from the Sky

Mel was a man of few words. Dressed in an orange overall and heavy army boots, he looked like an alien who had landed by mistake a few kilometers from the small town of Araguacema. He ran constantly between the hangar and his Cessna. On this day in November 1974, it took him over an hour to weigh and load each of the 17 boxes and cases I had brought along. Heavy parcels were stowed at the front of the plane, lighter ones at the rear. Mel was a meticulous man and, as I discovered later, took no risks. He never allowed me to help him in any way.

Having finished loading the plane, Mel went into the house to see if his wife had succeeded in establishing radio contact with missionaries working in other Kaiapo villages. Though she had just made contact with Iracema in the village of Gorotíre, it was difficult to understand what Iracema was saying. Radio contacts invariably were conducted in Portuguese in observance of the Brazilian government's ruling that radio operators had to converse in the national tongue. The combination of static and Mel and Iracema's American accents made it difficult for me to understand what Iracema was saying. I understood that the sky was clear over Gorotíre, although clouds were moving in quickly from the north. "We'll have to take off before the rains come," Mel muttered as he listened to Iracema's plea that he stop on his way back to pick up a sick child who required hospitalization. Mel said he would try to do so after leaving me with the Mekranoti.

I couldn't help noticing the scorn in Mel's voice. I knew he wasn't thrilled to be taking me to the Mekranoti. As a pilot of Asas de Socorro, a branch of the American Missionary Aviation Fellowship whose aim it was to assist missionaries working in the most remote areas of the globe, he had made it clear to me that he wasn't in the business of serving anthropologists. The only reason he was willing to make an exception was that I was armed with a rare but obligatory authorization from FUNAI (Fundação Nacional do Indio), the National Indian Foundation in Brasilia, as well as a request from that same governmental organization that he help me out. He was in no position to ignore a request from FUNAI, which sometimes refused the missionaries authorization to enter Indian villages.

Mel made no attempt to disguise the fact that he was not particularly hungry for my business. I regretted having had to come to him, but had had no choice. He was one of the few outsiders who knew the way to the Mekranoti, although he had made the trip only once before. "They are the most primitive of all Indians in this part of Brazil," he told me. On his previous visit, "all the men were painted in black and stood around my plane waving their long wooden clubs. I don't really trust them, especially now, since Jean [a missionary with the SIL (Summer Institute of Linguistics) who'd been working for years among the Kaiapo] is on holiday." I myself was concerned about Jean, whom I'd met some time before in Brasilia. She had been polite but totally uncooperative. Since she'd been stationed in the Mekranoti village for nearly two years now, I felt she might look on me as an intruder who might endanger her work.

While Mel tried to make radio contact with the missionaries working among the Kubenkrankênh, another Kaiapo group, his wife offered me a quick lunch of delicious home-made bread with butter and jam. "Enjoy it while you can," she said. "It will be some time before you eat anything like

this again." I didn't really grasp what she meant. All I wanted was to take off as soon as possible.

Mel was unable to make contact with the Kubenkrankênh village and seemed concerned, since it was the village closest to Mekranoti and therefore the best source of information about weather in the area. He nonetheless abruptly decided to take off. As we walked to the plane, he said, "Oh yes, there's one more thing. The trip has to be paid in advance, and there's no refund, even if we fail to land or to find the village." Weather appeared to be the main potential problem. If it rained too much, the grassy Mekranoti landing strip would be too slippery for landing; if there were too many clouds, it would be impossible to see the village from the air. I felt uncomfortable handing Mel a thousand dollars—pretty much all the cash I had—for a two-and-a-half-hour flight. He counted the cash, handed it to his wife, kissed her, prayed with her in front of the plane, and then urged me to board. Suddenly things seemed to be moving very fast.

Because I had so much luggage, Mel had removed all of the seats except his. He invited me to sit on one of my boxes. Having fastened our

The arrival of a plane always marks a welcome break in daily routine.

seat-belts, he started the engine and made a final instrument check. Suddenly we were in the air. Flying through low clouds, Mel leveled off below a second layer of clouds and headed northwest.

We were making for an area of clear sky. Below us lay the deep green of the Amazon jungle, which extends over more than 6,500,000 square kilometers, an area larger than all the countries of Europe (excluding Russia) combined. This immense forest still retained many of its secrets. Thousands of plant and animal species hadn't yet been identified, let alone studied, and a handful of Indian groups still roamed freely, seemingly without contact with the outside world. I knew all this, yet it was only in Mel's small single-engine plane, with this vast green carpet unrolling below us, that I hesitated. Why on earth had I come here? Were the Mekranoti really as frightening as Mel had said? More important, would they accept me?

Some 30 minutes later, I heard Iracema saying on the radio that the Gorotíre Indians had heard our plane. Mel pointed to a clearing ahead of us and banked to the left. Gradually, we moved away from Gorotíre, where I had in fact been for two weeks a couple of months earlier, during my first attempt to reach the Mekranoti. As the only Indian village to which the Brazilian Air Force maintained regular flights, Gorotíre—of all the Kaiapo villages—could be considered the most acculturated. The village was no longer laid out in the traditional circle, but was composed instead of several streets. Missionaries and government agents had been working there since the late 1930s. There was a school, and many Gorotíre wore western clothes, often leaving their bodies unpainted underneath. In addition, a lot of the younger men spoke Portuguese and no longer wore their hair long. Most anthropologists wanting to work among the Kaiapo started their research in Gorotíre, encouraged by the relative ease of communication with the outside world. While staying there, I'd been told that none of these facilities would be offered at Mekranoti. In a way this news had reassured me, because it suggested that I was heading for an isolated and therefore traditional group. Yet it also sounded quite frightening.

Flights from Gorotíre to Mekranoti had proven to be nonexistent. In a second attempt to reach Mekranoti, I had traveled north to the city of Belém. FUNAI agents in Brasilia had told me that a FUNAI flight was scheduled to leave soon; I was welcome to a free ride. Once again, this information proved totally spurious. Not only was no such flight scheduled but I also was told that I could never have flown on it. FUNAI personnel in Belém explained that flights to Mekranoti were so rare that on every occasion the plane was fully loaded with food and supplies for their local agents and the Indians. It was then that I learned about Mel. A missionary in Belém helped me out by checking with him about the cost of such a flight. I couldn't help noticing the smile on the missionary's face when he told me the amount. I'm sure he thought I'd give up. I certainly didn't have the money, having been in Brazil for months already. But I refused to give up and decided to return to São Paulo to arrange for some cash.

The trip to São Paulo, which I made by bus, proved to be one of the most uncomfortable journeys I've ever taken. Due to my limited finances, I purchased the cheapest possible ticket—there are different fare categories—first to Brasilia and then to São Paulo. On the first stretch, the bus stopped repeatedly and people jumped on and off, invariably loaded with sacks, chickens, and other unidentifiable items. Entire families seemed to be on the move. The sight of a "gringo" taking such a cheap ride aroused the curiosity of my fellow passengers. I wasn't alone for a minute. Occasionally, a band was formed with a few match-boxes, a couple of spoons, and a guitar. I participated in the singing, which sometimes lasted for over an hour. But not everything was this delightful. At one point a man sat down next to me who had lost his arm in a machine while working on the construction of the Transamazon Highway. During one of the many stopovers, a thief managed to steal the belongings of a man seated in front of me. On two occasions, the bus got stuck in the thick mud that delayed our schedule considerably. And during one long stopover, a woman offered me her 10-year-old daughter for a "modest payment," adding that the girl was "still a virgin." Instead of accepting, I invited mother and daughter to join me for a meal. The other passengers were astounded. How could I refuse such an engaging offer? And, worse still, why did I invite the woman and girl to eat with me?

Bôkre wearing his penis sheath
and carrying his painted son.

study the ground below us very carefully. As we followed the course of a small river, he banked to the left, to the right, then to the left again. "This is the Xixê River," he told me, "and somewhere over there I've got to spot a garden area before I can proceed any further." We were flying quite low, and I could see a pair of macaws gliding over the carpet of green cauliflowers. The Xixê seemed pretty minor to me. "Is this the river near which the Mekranoti live?" I asked. Mel said it wasn't, adding "You'll see that this is a big river. The Mekranoti live along the upper course of one of its affluents." Although I tried to follow the courses of a few of these affluents, they soon were swallowed by the greenness.

In the meantime, Mel had spotted his garden clearing. I hadn't seen him react as enthusiastically to anything before and dared to hope that his discovery meant a breakthrough in finding the village. He now turned the plane due west. Soon all signs of rivers and creeks had vanished. This made me feel uneasy, because I knew that in the infinity of the tropical rain forest, jungle pilots often relied solely on rivers to navigate. Mel stared attentively at the area in front of him. The landscape below us became more undulating. In the distance, a range of hills no more than two hundred meters high could be seen. I thought this must be the natural division between the watersheds of the Curuá and Xixê rivers, which dominate the area hydrographically, fed by a series of innumerable creeks and minor rivers that sprout in the hills and cross them on an east–west axis.

Some eight minutes later—it seemed like ages to me—we both spotted a series of insignificant clearings at the bottom of some hills. Since these were gardens, the village couldn't be much farther. Without saying a word, Mel pointed to his left. Behind the hills, I noticed a small swath in the forest. It was the landing strip with the Mekranoti village next to it. The village lay in a natural amphitheater with a semicircle of hills to the north and east and flatter, more open ground running to the south and west. It was only possible to see it from directly overhead. Mel circled over the two concentric rings of houses with a bare earth plaza in the middle and one hut at the center of the plaza. A number of people were standing on the plaza looking up at us, shielding their eyes with their hands;

The trip took nearly 60 hours. On arriving exhausted in São Paulo, I immediately sent messages to Belgium asking for financial help. Salvation arrived some three weeks later in the form of a small grant of the Leopold III Foundation. I now had the money to hire a plane to go to Mekranoti, but not a penny more. Indeed, there would be no money left to pay for the return flight, but at that point I didn't care at all.

The main thing was to get where I wanted to go. After more than two hours in the air, Mel began to

others were running to the landing strip. The scene reminded me of a famous picture taken in the 1940s that showed Xavánte Indians shooting arrows at a plane making a reconnaissance flight over their village.

Things happened very quickly. As Mel brought the plane down, the engine made terrible noises. The people standing at the opposite end of the airstrip and the wall of forest behind them seemed to be approaching at an alarming speed. Mel braked repeatedly and the plane shuddered until he finally managed to slow down and taxi up to the group of waiting Indians. The landing strip was slippery, and the weight of my luggage had only made things worse. Furthermore, the strip itself was only six hundred meters long. Having nonetheless landed safely, we were confronted by several Mekranoti. How was I supposed to greet them? I smiled and extended my hand, but received no response. The Indians closest to the plane were shouting at one another, while Mel was literally throwing my lug-gage out of it in his hurry to take off again as soon as possible. I just stood there, trying to imagine how I must look, a strange, pale anthropologist who'd descended from the sky—reminding me of a Kaiapo myth explaining how the Indians had lived in the heavens before descending to earth using an enormously long rope.

The Indians didn't seem as frightening as Mel had described them. This may have been due to the fact that the group consisted entirely of women and children. The adults were all dressed in western clothing. A seemingly important group of mostly elderly women remained at a distance, seated near the edge of the landing strip, staring motionless at the spectacle. The women and children around the plane tried to open my boxes. Mel came over, shook my hand, and wished me well. Waving at the Indians, he climbed back into his plane and took off again.

Suddenly, it was weirdly silent. Was it because I'd been cooped up for over two hours in a small

The interior of my house with my hammock, a platform to store luggage, and a kerosene lamp.

noisy plane or because the Indians were no longer shouting? I was disoriented until I realized that the constant buzz of urban life was nowhere in evidence.

A young man emerged from the forest, carrying his rifle and a curassow bird he'd killed. He said something to the women and then came over and shook my hand. I was relieved by this first sign of welcome. In Portuguese I started to ask about Marcos, the FUNAI agent I'd been told would be in the village. The man replied in Kaiapo. I only understood him when he pointed toward the north and repeated the word *Baú* several times. So Marcos was in Baú, a smaller village some 180 kilometers as the crow flies from where I'd landed! I'd been assured in Belém and Brasilia that although Mekranoti was isolated, I'd never be on my own, because missionaries and FUNAI agents would always be in the vicinity. Yet here I was, alone, and—lacking a radio—completely cut off from the outside world. And for how long?

Rooted to the spot, I tried to get hold of myself. Hoping to find out where the men of the village were, I asked "My?" The Indians laughed. I was puzzled. Had I used the wrong word? I repeated it several times, but was answered with general hilarity. (It was only later that I learned that the word *my* means penis. To refer to men properly, I should have asked "Memy?", meaning "people with a penis.")

Nobody seemed to grasp the idea that I hoped to be sheltered in the village. We all just stood there on the landing strip. It was about two o'clock in the afternoon and extremely hot. I sweated profusely, perspiration running down my chest and soaking my shirt. The air was saturated with moisture. Thick clouds seemed to presage a heavy rainfall —though it didn't rain that day.

The situation changed when a second man emerged from the forest. He too carried a rifle, as well as a machete and a bunch of green genipap fruits. This man, older than the first one, made a great impression on me, big and strong as he looked. Not knowing his name, in my mind I nicknamed him the Giant and the other man the Hunter. The Giant smiled at me and started talking loudly to the women, who responded and pointed with their lips toward the east, probably explaining where I had come from. Without hesitation, the Giant took up a heavy parcel from my luggage and strolled off toward the village. As if an order had been given, the other bystanders took the rest of my things and followed the Giant.

Everyone came to a halt in front of a big house on the outskirts of the village. Although the door had a lock on it, that didn't seem to bother the Giant, who used his machete to force it. My luggage was thrown into the house and I was urged to enter. I noticed that the house was usually inhabited by westerners; perhaps this was Marcos's house. The building was actually a rectangular thatched hut with a pitched roof and clay walls. A few openings in the walls served as windows. There were three fairly clean rooms, a rudimentary table with benches, and two platforms to serve as shelves. There was even a wash-bowl with a tap, connected by means of a plastic tube to a big water reservoir mounted behind the house. These were to be my quarters for the months to come.

I sat down on one of the benches and looked around me. About 50 women and children lingered in and around the house. Slowly, they seemed to relax. Some of the women smiled at me, others squatted on the ground and started delousing their children, and still others poked holes in the cardboard boxes I had brought with me. I'd heard descriptions of incessant stealing by Indians and hoped my things wouldn't be ransacked. An old woman came over to me. She was naked, had pendulous breasts and graying hair, and her left eye was closed. Her entire body was painted with irregular black motifs. Holding a long, thick pipe, she said something I couldn't understand. Since she repeated the sentence over and over again, I could only repeat it back to her. So "Nãr Bir Bir" was my first Kaiapo sentence. Although I didn't know it at that time, Bir Bir was the name the Mekranoti had given Jean, the missionary. So they were inquiring after Jean. As I repeated the woman's question, some of the other women roared with laughter. A few of them started saying other words or phrases, which I repeated. Pointing to myself, I said "Idji Gustávo." They tried to repeat my name, but in vain, since the letter "v" doesn't exist in Kaiapo and my name violated Kaiapo rules of vowel harmony. So my name was transformed into Gustába.

Since the women seemed to be enjoying themselves, I began pointing at individuals and asking

Bri (Mister Serious) and his ingenious wife in a forest camp.

their names. In most Amerindian societies, a series of taboos governs the saying of names, especially one's own name, so neighbors responded for one another. Perhaps I was being encouraged to repeat outrageous things rather than names, because the laughter became louder and louder. I didn't care.

After a while, the women left. As the house emptied, I took advantage of this first moment of relative tranquillity to move my luggage into one of the rooms which had a door. This was more a symbolic gesture than anything else, since the door had no lock. I also unpacked my hammock. Since I saw no mosquitoes, I decided not to hang my mosquito net. Trying to unravel the hammock strings, I looked for a place to hang it. A young boy with curly hair who'd stayed behind took the hammock from me, unraveled the strings in a flash, and hung it up under the supervision of a man who'd entered the house without my having seen him. Because of his serious expression, I nicknamed him Mister Serious. It was only much later that I understood that he had reasons to be somber. In Kaiapo society, senior men are expected to have reached the

highest status within the community. Since Mister Serious had no legitimate children and was not renowned for his knowledge or for a particular skill, he was shown little respect.

Later that afternoon, another man arrived. I heard him coming from far away as he shouted his way through the crowd of women and children which had begun to assemble again in and around my house. I nicknamed this man Al Capone, not only because he immediately struck me as a man with authority but also because, in addition to his western shirt, shorts, and hat, he wore sunglasses, a few cheap chains around his neck, and a belt with bullets and a revolver. He spoke to me in a serious and assertive manner, but as before, all I could do was smile. He paused, looked right into my eyes, and began to laugh. He then spoke humorously to the others in the house and squatted next to Mister Serious.

Though I didn't eat that evening, I enjoyed having a handful of people sitting in my house. This was my first opportunity to observe them. The Giant was there, wearing a palm leaf made

14

Irekangro carrying her baby in a sling.

Portuguese words for such highly coveted trade goods as pots, pans, machetes, glass beads, hammocks, ammunition, scissors, and so on. I found the cut tobacco I'd brought and gave him some. Having tasted it, he passed his pipe to his neighbors. They appeared to discuss the quality or taste of the tobacco, but since the senior men never asked for it again, I realized this wasn't the type of tobacco they wanted. Only the adolescents liked it because, following western habits, they occasionally rolled cigarettes. The older people clearly preferred the strong black tobacco they kept in thick rolls and smoked in their pipes.

When everyone finally left, I shut the door and crawled into my hammock. Finding it incredibly uncomfortable on my back, I tried to turn on my side. The hammock capsized, and I fell out onto the ground. How could people say they enjoyed sleeping in hammocks? Crawling back into it, I finally discovered that if I lay diagonally I could lie flat and also move around as much as I wished. Why had no-one told me this?

That night I hardly slept. I couldn't become accustomed to the oppressive silence. Actually, it wasn't really silence. The night was filled with sounds I didn't recognize. I heard crickets and frogs, but also unidentifiable creatures. There was the distant yet friendly buzz of conversation and snoring. An occasional outburst of laughter or dog's bark brought life to the darkness. Toward the east I heard a bizarre noise, low and persistent, which stopped frequently only to start up again. I thought it might be jaguars, but later discovered that the sound was produced by a band of howler monkeys. Running through the fascinating incidents of the past 12 hours in my mind, I was puzzled by the lack of men in the village. Were they on a seasonal migration into the forest? And where was the man I'd been told about in the city, who was supposed to be quite fluent in Portuguese and who lived in this village? Unable to answer these questions, I finally fell asleep.

Early the next morning, I was awakened by knocking on my door. I quickly climbed out of my hammock; as I opened the door, I was greeted by the early morning chill, and a thick haze entered the room. Three naked women stood there with big empty baskets on their backs. The dresses they'd worn the day before apparently had been put away.

into a cone over his penis—typical Kaiapo men's dress and also the Indians' sole traditional form of clothing. Next to the Giant sat a man with a wooden disk in his lower lip. He struck me as calm and accommodating, barely saying a word, listening to the conversations of the others, carefully observing every move I made. He constantly held his pipe in a corner of his mouth. After a while, he gently said "Karinhô." When I failed to respond, he said, in Portuguese, "Tobacco!" This was my very first step in learning Kaiapo. As it became clear to me later, most of the men and a few of the women knew the

The women just looked at me. As far as I could tell, they didn't have a particular reason to wake me, other than curiosity. Or did they think I should be up, since it was already 6:00 a.m.? Two of the women carried children in woven slings. As I admired the beautiful painting on their bodies, one of the women saw my box of matches lying on the table. Ignoring me, she entered the house, took the matches, and left. As the other women withdrew, I heard all three of them giggle. The event preoccupied me. How could I prevent people from taking anything they wanted from me? I had to figure out how to prevent this, but as long as I couldn't express myself, I didn't see how I could deal with the problem. I knew that learning the Mekranoti language was an absolute priority, but the question was how to achieve this goal—preferably as fast as possible. I felt handicapped, dumb, and isolated. I knew that the few westerners who'd spent time with the Mekranoti had either worked in other Kaiapo communities before acquiring a basic knowledge of the language, or used interpreters they'd brought with them. For better or worse, I was the first outsider to arrive without such "baggage."

As before, there were visitors throughout the second day, and I wasn't left alone for a single minute. I couldn't tell whether I was being spied on or whether my recreational value kept people coming. The Mekranoti seemed to enjoy the unpredictability of my actions. That day, I saw a series of new faces. I was especially interested in two of the men. The first was an old man who arrived with an axe over his shoulder and wearing the traditional penis sheath. He had an imposing physique and, while fairly old for a Mekranoti, was still vigorous. Taller than most Kaiapo I'd seen, he had an extremely solemn face. I behaved with him as I had with all the others. He remained in the doorway rather than entering my house. When one of the boys whispered "Cacique," the Portuguese word for "chief," I realized that the man was Beprôrôk, the village chief. Now I recognized him from a picture I'd seen in a book and from a TV documentary that had been made two years earlier. Moving toward him, I said his name. He looked surprised—was it because I knew his name or because I'd said it just like that out in the open?—and for a moment he stared at me. I was afraid I'd just committed a major blunder. Ashamed, I turned aside, but then he put

Chief Beprôrôk.

his hand on my shoulder and smiled. Feeling reassured, I mentioned the name of his wife, which I had read in a census in the FUNAI office in Brasilia. His smile became even more expressive. The idea that his name was known to a total stranger seemed to impress him. After speaking to the women and children gathered in my house, he left.

The other man I'd noticed turned out to be Krujêt, a white man who'd been taken captive in 1918 when he was about three. Like Beprôrôk one of the oldest people in the village, he'd formerly worn a big wooden lip disk, but had removed it a few years previously, leaving a large gap in his lower lip through which saliva dripped constantly. Quite slender, he was unlike the Indians. His skin was like sandpaper, and he had red-brown curly hair. The boy with the curly black hair who'd helped me hang my hammock the day before proved to be his youngest son. Unlike most of the other men, who spoke assertively, Krujêt usually spoke with a high, nagging intonation. That day he stayed for hours, making himself some sort of interlocutor as people arrived to see me. Krujêt did most of the talking, apparently explaining my actions and reactions to the others. At midday,

I prepared some soup and ate a few bananas Krujêt had given me. As the days passed, he looked after me, in the beginning bringing burning firewood each morning and seeing to it that the fire kept burning for the entire day.

My anthropology professor in Europe, Simone Dreyfus, had taught me that anthropology was the science of patience. She knew of several anthropologists who wanted to start working or taking pictures the minute they'd arrived in the field. This had often led to tension, and in some cases the communities in question had indicated that the anthropologists' presence wasn't appreciated at all. I didn't want this to happen to me and so had decided to let people come to me before I went to them with my endless questions. I also didn't take any pictures in the beginning, although I always had my camera on hand, so that everyone would become accustomed to it.

As an anthropologist, I'd come to observe the Mekranoti in order to understand aspects of their social life. During the first days and weeks, however, I was the one being observed—thoroughly, obsessively, endlessly. I therefore had to find a balance between being observed and having the free-dom to move around without being followed. My first steps in this direction involved occasionally stepping out of the house just to stretch my legs, feel the sun, or catch a glimpse of the village less than 50 meters away. I didn't wander farther than 20 meters or so from my house. There were these inevitable moments when I had to leave the house and my luggage unattended, for instance when I went into the forest to relieve myself. Although no-one followed me on these occasions, even then I was being watched, at least sometimes. Once I was surprised in the forest by a grinning adolescent boy. Covering my privates with my hands, I grinned foolishly. Seeing a naked John Cleese surprised by unexpected visitors 15 years later in *A Fish Called Wanda* reminded me of how I'd felt that day in the Amazon jungle. When the Mekranoti boy realized I'd seen him, he disappeared.

I often felt imprisoned, even though it was a prison I'd created myself. Although I'd brought some books with me, I refrained from reading. The distance between, say, the world of Hercule Poirot and the one in which I found myself was so huge that I couldn't seem to bridge it. Trying to escape the feeling that I was being constantly watched,

A view of the Mekranoti village with the platforms on which meat, tobacco, and annatto seeds are dried in the sun.

I tried to nap in my hammock. People invariably came by, knocking on the door or rocking the hammock. Many would keep shouting until I reacted, while others behaved more discreetly and merely peered through my windows. If they saw I was alone, they'd start calling out to me, however.

Privacy in the sense I understood it was a concept the Indians didn't seem to acknowledge or respect. It wasn't difficult to see why. In their society, almost everything is done in the open. While I felt the lack of privacy to be the most painful part of my experience, I knew I had to adopt to the Mekranoti way of life. As yet, I was merely a passive part of the Indians' surroundings; my role was limited to one of distraction, helping, giving, and—above all—being on call 24 hours a day! Sometimes I'd be awakened in the night by people who seemed simply to have come to ask me something.

I decided that I needed to move about and do something and resolved to have a daily walk. The question was where to walk to. The only place I knew of was the landing strip, and since I wasn't ready to push my luck by entering the village, the landing strip became my destination. There, I walked up and down for about half an hour almost every afternoon, outings I very much enjoyed. I saw birds and lizards, as well as other small animals. Once I even saw a large snake, which I later identified as a Bushmaster, the most venomous reptile in the Amazon jungle. At times, a man would cross the landing strip on his return from a hunt, and after staring at me for a moment—what on earth was I doing there all by myself?—he'd continue to the village. These were serene moments for me, the most peaceful ones I had—in fact my only moments of privacy.

During my brief absences, I left my door unlocked; since the lock had been forced, I had little choice. For the first few days, I felt uncomfortable about leaving people in the house while I went out for my stroll. When I returned, I could always see that the Indians had been opening my luggage. Although in a way this didn't really bother me, since most of the things I'd brought were meant for them anyway, I did worry about stealing. As far as I could tell, nothing was ever taken, though, and this made me feel more comfortable.

The need to bathe presented itself very early on. It was the rainy season, and although I hadn't

yet experienced rain in the jungle myself, the air was sultry. And I was dirty. I also needed drinking water, since I didn't trust the quality of the water in the reservoir; when I checked it, I discovered that it was filled with dead insects and even a bird. So when I saw my female neighbor Big Smile wandering toward the village with a pot in her hand, I grabbed my own pot and a towel and followed her, hoping that she wouldn't stop at one of the houses for a visit. She didn't. As I followed her, I heard voices coming from the different houses. Were people calling out to me? I wasn't really sure, and so I smiled and responded in Portuguese. This seemed to be acceptable to some of the women, but not to others. Later on, when I'd begun to gain some fluency in the Kaiapo language, I realized that many of the women thought that Portuguese was an uncivilized language and refused to speak it at all.

I finally reached the bathing place. The water was quite high, but had not yet reached its highest level; the rainy season was just beginning. Numerous children were playing in the water, climbing and jumping from a big tree that stood alone on the opposite bank. A few women were sitting around and chatting while they washed and ate sweet potatoes. All were naked. I undressed and entered the

Small Akamàn, who from the very beginning spent much of his time in and around my house.

18

water. I couldn't help noticing that all eyes were focused on me and that the same range of responses I'd noted before was set off, with some women laughing and others responding negatively. However, I'd begun to see that normal Kaiapo speech might sound excited and angry to someone unfamiliar with its strongly stressed syllables and exaggerated stops. When people were agitated or discussing something in a group, they might therefore sound domineering. So on that occasion at the river, I didn't pay much attention to the seemingly harsh way some of the women spoke to me. I smiled politely at everyone who addressed me, whatever their tone of voice. However, since one older woman kept shouting, I wondered whether perhaps she wanted some of my soap or if I, as a man, wasn't allowed to bathe when women were around. I therefore considered the possibility that a separate bathing place existed for the men, as so often seemed to be the case among Amazon Indian groups. I offered the woman my soap, but when she refused and left the bathing place, I became convinced that I'd transgressed some rule of the group.

The next day, I tried to find out when one of the few men present in the village would head toward the river, so that I'd be sure not to make the same mistake again. To my surprise, a man I'd nicknamed Big Lip-Disk went to the same bathing place as the women. No one paid particular attention to him, but whenever I went to bathe, a group of women and children invariably appeared. Only much later, when I could speak some Kaiapo, was I told that the women had followed me in order to be able to look at my penis. Kaiapo men always wore a penis sheath or pair of shorts, so while some of the women (the elderly ones) were upset by my shameless behavior, others profited from these occasions. Once I realized that it was inappropriate for a man to bathe entirely naked, I refrained from doing so, except on rare occasions during forest trips when only men were around. As soon as I stopped, I ceased being an object of curiosity at the riverside.

I was glad to find that there were far fewer big night mosquitoes (the ones I knew from Europe) here than in Gorotíre. There were many more of the smaller variety, though, the ones that attack during the day. Normally, I barely felt it when they bit me, but soon an irritated small red dot would appear. At night, when the temperature fell, these spots became very itchy, and I'd start scratching them, often in my sleep. The unpleasant result was frequent infections, especially around my ankles. After a few days, my hands were covered with bites. Due to the constant biting and resulting irritation, my hands often trembled, and at times I had some difficulty writing. The Indians seemed to be bothered as much as I was by these obnoxious mosquitoes; the skin on their backs, for instance, was as rough as coarse sandpaper. I now understood why most women often wore dresses, and why most men donned shirts whenever any were available.

As if it wasn't enough to be harassed by these bugs, I was also bothered by another type of even smaller insect, a red tick that thrived in the damp grass. When I walked through the grass, ticks jumped onto my legs, where they nestled under the skin. The result was similar to that produced by mosquito bites. Because the ticks were so tiny, it took a while before I discovered what was producing the infernal itching. At first I tried to remove them with a needle, but soon found that this procedure only resulted in infection. Later, I tried using mercurochrome, which did indeed chase the ticks away, but I often had the impression that they simply moved to another part of my body. Moreover, I looked extremely foolish with all these red dots all over my legs. I imagined that wearing long trousers might deter the ticks, but soon discovered that this only made matters worse, since even more ticks were attracted by my damp trouser legs.

It must have been the eighth or ninth day of my stay when Uneven Breast (so nicknamed by me because her left breast was considerably smaller than her right one) and her son entered my house. When she spoke to me, all I could do was say in Portuguese how much I regretted not being able to understand a word. Over and over again she repeated the same short phrases. Krujêt, who was, as always, in attendance, came to my rescue, at first simply repeating what the woman had said while she stared at me as if I were deaf. I remained quiet and smiled. A hopeless idiot, she must have thought. Finally, Krujêt took a small white stick and pointed to the boy's buttocks. "Teprãndjà," he said. I understood what was meant: the child had worms. I went into what I referred to as the bedroom and, watched by Krujêt and a few others who had assembled, I opened a box filled with medicines.

Taking out a tablet of the appropriate medicine, I gave it to the woman, gesturing to indicate that the boy had to come back the next morning.

The next day, when the boy returned for his second tablet in a course of six, I reckoned that his condition had improved, because suddenly everybody seemed to be in desperate need of medicine. The Indians had decided that I must be a doctor. Recently contacted Indians invariably suffer from newly imported illnesses such as smallpox, measles, flu, and even simple colds against which they have no resistance and which can wipe out entire groups in just a few days. Adequate medical assistance was therefore always needed. In no time, my house turned into a jungle pharmacy. All day long, people would come to get medicines, sometimes returning again the same day. Communication remained a major obstacle, though. In the beginning, the women would just yell the names of their illnesses (or those of their children) at me. My ignorant response would cause irritation until someone— usually Krujêt or a woman who'd already been through the routine—explained that gestures were more efficient than shrieks. I was lucky that no serious disease had to be treated during the weeks that followed. Mostly, people complained of headaches

and intestinal disorders. Fortunately—and also as a precautionary measure—I'd brought an impressive amount of medicine for such ills and was therefore able to help most of my "patients." To the others, I merely gave vitamins, letting psychology do the rest. Some insisted on having injections, which I was unable to provide. However, I glossed over this deficiency by offering effervescent tablets of vitamin C. The ritual of having to wait until the bubbles had vanished seemed to suggest that these were strong medicine, and even today, nearly 20 years later, the Mekranoti still talk about my antidotes to muscle aches and intestinal disorders.

I took advantage of the situation not only to learn the names and descriptions of all common diseases and bodily infirmities but also to learn people's names. On index cards, I phonetically noted the names of all my "patients," the descriptive nicknames I used as an aide-memoire, and the treatments they received. In the beginning, people often gave false names. When they returned, I would whisper these names to them, only to discover that they were incorrect. Although bystanders seemed to enjoy this, the "patients" themselves apparently didn't, insisting that someone in the group say their correct names for me. After a few

The black genipap dye is applied with a fine palm-rib stylet. Line by line, a fine and intricate geometrical design materializes.

Bepkô watches me copying a body painting on a sheet of paper. A young leader when this picture was taken, he later became a chief.

weeks, I was certain that I had nearly the entire adult population in my card index, at least those present in the village. I still hadn't figured out where the rest of the men were, however.

My diet at this time was far from variable, consisting solely of rice, spaghetti, and, above all, soups and canned food (corned beef, sausages, vegetables, tomato puree) that I'd brought with me. Since I always gave the leftovers to visitors, certain people "happened" to drop by whenever I was eating, hardly ever entering the house on other occasions. The Mekranoti ate my food with great pleasure, except for spaghetti, to which they reacted disapprovingly by saying "Teprãndjà!" I'd found the only meal I could have in total peace.

After about a month or so, I began to realize that my food supplies were diminishing at an alarming speed. Uncertainty began to weigh on me. While the Indians had brought me small numbers of bananas (usually handfuls of half-rotten leftovers), I couldn't live exclusively on them. I started hating myself for having brought so many gifts for the Indians and far too little food. Survival seemed more important than these tens of kilos of knives, machetes, glass beads, ammunition, and so on that I had stacked in my room! I started eating less and sometimes clandestinely late at night, so I wouldn't feel obliged to share my food with visitors. As the days passed, I became obsessed with the idea that I had to find food. I thought of standing in front of my house waiting for the women to come back from their gardens with loads of sugar cane, bananas, sweet potatoes, and manioc and offering them a knife or something else in exchange. Although the idea seemed attractive, I realized that once the news got around, I might suddenly be brought large amounts of food I wouldn't be able to use in exchange for trade goods. I was as yet in no position to accept something from one person and refuse the same thing from another. Another possibility was to follow a few women to their gardens and try to beg some produce from them. But how would people react to me following women to their gardens? I knew that recently contacted Indians such as the Mekranoti didn't appreciate strange men following their women to isolated places in the forest.

As I continued to try to figure out a solution to this apparently dead-end situation, a major event occurred. Beprôrôk, the old chief of whom I'd seen very little, came to my house one day and, without saying a word, took me by the arm and guided me to his house. There, he urged me to sit on a wooden block. This was the first time I'd entered a Mekranoti house. It was quite dark inside. Banana skins and other "dishes" were scattered about on the floor, attracting clouds of flies and other insects. There were two doors and no windows (in theory to prevent flies and mosquitoes from entering during the day and to keep the warmth in at night). While Beprôrôk sat on his bench across from me, his wife, Ronkà, handed me a piece of manioc bread with some slices of meat. Having eaten everything, I stayed as long as I could, for I enjoyed having been invited to enter a house and given a meal. In all, I counted six beds at Beprôrôk's. The Kaiapo traditionally didn't have hammocks. Until recently, in fact, they'd been considered "marginal peoples," because—unlike the majority of neighboring groups—they didn't know how to make canoes or ceramic pots and hadn't learned to weave cotton, or at least to use their skills to produce textile goods such as clothing or hammocks. Six nuclear families—about twenty-five or thirty people—lived in Beprôrôk's large house. Some of the beds were rudimentary wooden platforms, while others merely consisted of palm leaves and woven mats on the ground. Fires had been laid between the beds; personal belongings were stored in bags, baskets, and sacks around the sleeping places. As I sat there, people went in and out. Nobody seemed to be bothered by my presence.

Across the room, I noticed the boy I'd cured of worms being painted by his mother. I gestured to Beprôrôk that I wanted to watch what she was doing. Pointing with his lips, he urged me to do so. Pleased that the chief had understood me, I moved over to watch the woman, whose real name turned out to be Nokàjabjê. My presence didn't seem to bother her at all, which also pleased me. After a while, she looked over at me to see if I was still watching her work. Kaiapo women take great pride in their painting skills, and it was easy to understand why. While the boy lay on a mat, half asleep, Nokàjabjê patiently ran the fine, flexible palm-rib stylus stained with black dye from a genipap fruit over his body. She proceeded gently and accurately. Applied line by line, an intricate geometric design materialized. Genipap body painting is more informational than expressive, providing data on the individual's life cycle, age and sex, and social relationships, and about issues of reciprocity and hierarchy. It is also the foremost expression of perfection and beauty in Kaiapo society. Gradually, as the boy's body was covered with paint, I realized that a sort of garment was being created for him.

I noted a remarkable difference between the Nokàjabjê I'd seen in and around my house and the person sitting here painting her son. While in public she displayed the assertive and confident aspects of her personality, within her own household she was extremely gentle, friendly, and caring. As I was to find out, this was true of most Kaiapo women. Sitting there, I suddenly realized that I'd discovered a means of communicating with all of them: through the art of body painting. This seemed an excellent way of interacting with the women without making too much of my reasons for observing them. So, whenever a woman came to visit me, I showed particular interest either in her own body painting or in that of her children, asking the names of motifs and sometimes even copying them on paper. The women loved to watch me do this and seemed to enjoy the way I reproduced two-dimensionally a painting that should've been applied to a body. Since the women often asked me to give them knives, razor blades, or scissors, I tried to explain through gestures that they could have these in exchange for body-painting motifs drawn on paper. Initially, I wanted to give them pencils, but they refused to use them. Fortunately, as it turned out, they preferred to take the paper home and work with their own natural dyes. This worked well on both sides, and communication seemed to improve. No longer the "doctor" locked up in his "hospital," I became instead a doctor interested in the culture of his "patients." One important side-effect of this strategy was that I could now go and visit the women in their homes to give them paper, fetch drawings, or bring them the gifts they wanted in exchange. The doors of the village had finally opened to me. This was, of course, primarily due to Beprôrôk's first invitation. As the oldest man in the village, he'd shown his community that I could be trusted.

In 1974, the Mekranoti village consisted of a circle of houses that had been built in the late 1960s and a second circle of houses built later to shelter the growing population, including newcomers from other Mekranoti villages. The men's house was located in the middle of the central plaza. Houses occupied by missionaries and FUNAI agents could be identified easily from the air because of their lighter-colored roofs. Since the Indians keep fires going constantly in their houses, even relatively new houses have blackened roofs. Major paths from the village lead to the bathing site along the river and to gardens and hunting sites.

For strategic reasons, traditional Kaiapo villages are located near low mountains. In 1978, the Mekranoti rebuilt their village so that all houses formed a single big circle. The new village looked impressive, and the Indians were proud of it, since traditional Kaiapo villages were said to have been occupied by over two thousand inhabitants. The Mekranoti spoke with nostalgia of the times when their populations were much larger.

New houses are easily recognizable by their clean roofs and, if they've only just been constructed, by their walls made of palm leaves. These are later replaced by wooden frames filled in with clay.

The interior of a Mekranoti house always has all sorts of leaves and other garbage on the floor. The women try to clean their houses at least once a day to keep down the insect population. Big houses lived in by numerous women often are cleaner than others occupied by one or two, since the latter often have little or no time to do anything other than care for their offspring. In recent years, mosquito nets have become coveted trade goods. Although most Mekranoti now have hammocks, many still prefer to sleep on wooden platforms.

Children spend much of their time playing in the plaza, imitating the activities of the adults, shooting with bows and arrows at fruits or lizards, playing soccer with fiber balls they make themselves, and so on. By the time boys reach the age of six or eight, they'll have formed cliques of close friends who start venturing into the area behind the houses or playing for hours in the river.

In the late afternoon, the women usually gather in front of
their houses, watching the plaza while keeping an eye on their
children. With few mosquitoes around and a pleasant temperature, this is by far the most enjoyable time of the day.

Normally, village women avoid the center of the plaza or,
more precisely, the men's house. They're only allowed to
enter or approach the men's house under specific ritual
circumstances. In order to catch a man's attention for any
reason, a woman may either send a child or approach the
men's house and call to him from a safe distance. Children
are allowed to move freely within the village and even enter
houses other than their own without being invited. Adults
will only do so when invited, or they'll approach slowly,
announcing their arrival and asking for the person with
whom they wish to speak.

On returning from daily work in the gardens, the women usually gather by the river to bathe and chat. Deprived of an institutional meeting place like the men's house, they hold spontaneous meetings at the river to discuss village politics and decide about group activities.

Like most forest people, the Mekranoti are quite keen on their looks. They bathe at least twice a day, occasions used by women and girls to collect fresh water to take back to their houses. Babies and small children are usually carried by their mothers in woven slings, thus leaving both hands free for work.

Nokàjabjê in the plaza carrying two of her children. She's a strong-willed woman, very attentive to her offspring and close relatives, but harsh to anyone who interferes with her family's interests.

Children usually wear the most ornaments in Mekranoti villages, invariably including beaded earrings and armlets. Senior children often make palm-leaf headbands for themselves and their junior siblings as a way of learning how to manufacture ornaments. This particular type of headband is one the Mekranoti learned from the neighboring Suia Indians during their first encounters in the early twentieth century.

Irekum—one of the last men to wear a wooden lip disk—smoking his pipe. All his siblings having died in epidemics in the early 1950s, Irekum was the last surviving member of his family. Deprived of any close kin, he'd adopted Tàkàkmê, one of the village's ritual leaders and a contemporary of his, as his inseparable friend. The two men went hunting and fishing together, sat in the men's house together, and so on. Irekum had been a fierce warrior and was one of two Mekranoti men known to have occasional attacks of madness. Grabbing any available weapon, he'd threaten anyone in his vicinity, and the Indians would hide in their houses. Eventually, Irekum would disappear into the forest, returning as if nothing had happened a few days later. When he had a less violent outburst, Tàkàkmê—and only Tàkàkmê—was able to calm Irekum down.

Young Kôkôba with the typical decorations of his age grade. His head is shaven in the *jôkàr* style, he's painted with red and black paint, and he's wearing a new necklace of buttons and dark blue glass beads. In addition, he has beaded ear and lip ornaments, the latter being the precursor of the wooden lip disk he'd have worn when older if this custom was still followed.

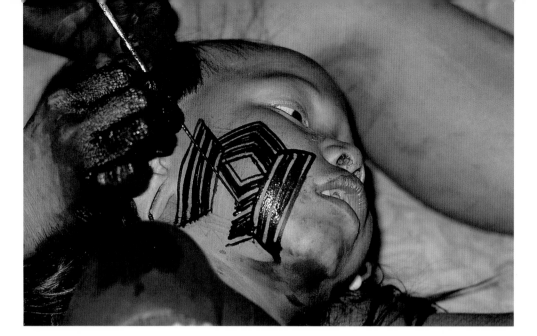

Nojaka's cheeks being painted with a palm-leaf stylus and black paint made of genipap pulp and pits chewed and mixed with charcoal, saliva, and water. Depending on the amounts of water and saliva and on the age of the fruit, such paintings remain visible on the skin for between eight and fourteen days.

Both younger and older children are almost invariably painted with fine motifs, while adults, normally painted with the same substance applied with the hands, "wear" clumsier motifs. On ritual occasions, adults and adolescents may also be embellished with fine motifs. Here, Kôkônhy is shown ready to act as a ritual friend during a naming ceremony.

In Mekranoti society, the moon is the symbol of fertility. All major rituals end with a full moon, not only so that all-night dancers can benefit from its pleasant glow but also because the moon is associated with new beginnings. It also symbolizes the cycle of passing time, growth, development, and serenity.

Getting Settled

Old Wajanga, with his lip disk and penis sheath, and Roiti participate in a dance of the naming ceremony of "the painted men."

Returning to my house from Beprôrôk's that evening, I wondered about his unexpected yet welcome invitation. In fact, as he told me later, men who'd examined my luggage during my outings had noticed that my food supplies were running out. Since I was helping them out with medicines, Beprôrôk thought he and his people should provide me with food. Falling asleep as I thought about how things seemed to be improving, I was re-awakened by the sound of shotguns. Putting my sandals on quickly, I ran out of the house toward the village. What could have happened? Had someone killed a jaguar or pig in the village? Was a fight going on? Surely, the Mekranoti weren't being attacked, since they had peaceful relations with all their traditional enemies. Arriving in the village, I found it quiet. The few people still awake, seemingly puzzled by my appearance, asked what was the matter. I mimed the shooting and sounds of a gun. The only parts I understood of the brief explanation I received were the name Wajanga and the word for "child."

Next morning, old Wajanga was one of my first visitors, wearing a penis sheath and a straw hat. A medium-sized lip disk trembled in his lower lip. Of all the men I'd seen with lip disks, Wajanga was the only one who seemed to have difficulty preventing his from shaking. Coming over to me, he took me by the arm and guided me to his house—the biggest one in the village. There, he proudly introduced me to his wife, who'd just had a daughter. I realized then that the shots of the night before had had something to do with the birth of the child. As it turned out, whenever a child is born among the Mekranoti, the father is supposed to fire his gun into the air to let the whole community know: two shots for a girl, three for a boy. Explaining the discrepancy, the Mekranoti say that one more shot is discharged for a boy because he will, when grown up, have to use the gun himself. Small bags are made for newborn children in which their umbilical cords and first ornaments are stored, constituting a sort of record of their growth. Three such pouches are made for girls, two for boys. Here, the difference is explained by the fact that girls, on growing up, will have to carry more baskets than boys.

The same day, Bri (the man I'd nicknamed Mister Serious) arrived with a parcel which he smilingly—an exceptional sight!—handed to me. Never having seen him smile before, I knew something was going on. Opening the green banana leaves, I was surprised to find a fish head. Bri and some others urged me to eat it, eyes and all, which I proceeded to do, noting that I was being observed attentively. Why on earth had I been given this head? When I'd finished, the Indians started talking again, and Bri asked me for a small knife. Surely, this fish head was not worth that much—maybe it was a delicacy among the Mekranoti?—but none-theless I gave Bri a knife. I later found out that the gift of the fish head had been a test. The FUNAI agents, the Mekranoti knew, mostly lived on their own provisions, and missionaries ate just about anything the rain forest—that is, the Indians—pro-vided. On their rare visits, members of medical teams only accepted the best cuts of meat. My situ-ation seemed to puzzle the Mekranoti. I'd come on a missionary plane, but they'd already found out I was no missionary, so they took me for a medical aid. Since no doctor had ever stayed for such a long time, they thought perhaps I was a nurse. Yet the only nurses they knew were from FUNAI. In order to clarify my identity (and my needs), the Mekranoti decided to test me in order to see how far I'd go in eating their food. I was given a fish head, something they knew westerners rarely ate. Since I ate it all, they were convinced that I'd eat just about any-thing, just like the missionaries. I was never given a fish head again, but from that day on, people started bringing me food. Not too much, not too little, just enough to survive. Nokàjabjê was the first to appear, bringing a perfect bunch of bananas.

A few days later, just before noon, the village suddenly became very noisy. People were yelling; some of the women wailed loudly. I ran to see what had happened and was surprised to find the house at the very center of the village filled with men. As I approached the men's house shyly, I discerned angry looks on many of the men's faces. At least 40 of them, young and old, were sitting on logs. Women stood around, their wailing intended as greetings for the returning men. In the midst of this highly emotional scene, one young man stood up and began talking while glancing at me. The women and the few men I already knew responded. Appar-ently, the newly arrived men were asking who I was. After some discussion and occasional laughter, the young man came over to me and asked, in Portu-guese, "Where's the coffee?" Finally, I thought, the

Nhàkmeti carrying a newborn baby to the river for its first symbolic bath. She also carries two small mats that later will be folded into small bags to protect the umbilical cord and the child's first ornaments.

man I had heard about had arrived! Having lived for more than two months without really being able to talk to anyone, I was exhilarated. My inability to communicate had begun to frighten me.

Although I very much wanted to stay to observe the arriving men, I thought it would be bet-ter for me to withdraw and prepare some coffee. I told the young man that it would be ready in an hour or so. About two hours later, a group of men arrived at my house. It was clear that they all had taken a bath before visiting me. The Portuguese-speaking man was among them. I set out the five cups I had, filled them with coffee, and proceeded to hand them around. The scene reminded me of my first day in Mekranoti, with people talking loudly, yelling questions or statements at me, and sticking their noses in all my belongings.

I greeted the Portuguese-speaking man, asking where the group of men had come from. He replied in Kaiapo. I tried another question, and once again he responded in Kaiapo. Was this Kenti, the man who was supposed to be fluent in Portuguese? He clearly understood what I said, but seemed inca-pable of answering in Portuguese. I felt even more isolated than before. Depressed, I sat down on a bench and realized that, at this speed, it would take me at least another six months in the field to gain some fluency in the native tongue. I definitely had made some progress; I knew the names of many objects, for instance, but these had been very easy to learn, since all I had to do was point to them and ask what they were called. It was different with verbs and adjectives. How could I communicate my feelings with gestures? Although mimicry is a universal phenomenon, gestures are interpreted in different ways in different societies. How could I express the idea that something was good or bad, friendly or hostile, slow or fast, warm or cold? How could I express the concepts of few or many? I'd already discovered that the Mekranoti have different words or expressions for concepts I wasn't accustomed to distinguishing. This discovery had convinced me that a thorough knowledge of the language was essential to my research. Feeling frustrated, I asked the young man "Kenti, how does one say 'hungry' in your language?" He stared at me, laughed, and—using his extremely limited Portuguese—explained that Kenti would be coming later, together with Marcos! I felt both relieved and frustrated, because I knew that "later" might mean tomorrow or next month.

Luckily, Marcos and a handful of other men arrived soon after that. I met Marcos first, greeting him enthusiastically, but my excitement soon dwindled due to his extreme aloofness. He immediately demanded to see my authorization—which I quickly fetched—and inquired about my intentions. When had I ordered the plane to come and pick me up again? How was I doing with food supplies? Guiding me to his house across the village from mine—so I wasn't sleeping in Marcos's house after all!—he began to lecture me on how difficult the Indians were or could be, on what a fool I was to come to Mekranoti without speaking a word of their language, and on the urgent need for more food supplies or else we'd both suffer a lot.

I was bewildered by Marcos's arrogance. On a piece of paper, he jotted down all the essential data mentioned on my authorization, saying "So, you're planning on staying here for a long time, are you? Well, I wish you luck. I just don't understand how the administration in the capital could grant authorization to such an inexperienced guy to work in one of the most remote villages in this part of the Amazon!" Without saying anything further, he walked into the bushes behind his house, where he started a motor connected by a few wires to the radio transmitter in his house. I was shocked to see that there'd been a radio in the village all the time; I was also stunned by the obnoxious noise of the engine, which seemed so alien and disturbing. Marcos tried in vain to contact Altamira or Belém, grumbling that it was too early and that he'd have to try again in the afternoon.

Things improved slightly when I invited Marcos to my house for coffee. After the third cup, he seemed to soften up, chatting more cordially and tackling the topic of isolation, which seemed to weigh on him as much as it did on me. "The only ways to contact the outside world are by radio or plane," he said. It seemed that FUNAI only rarely sent a plane to the village, and that was why none of Marcos's colleagues were eager to work there. All preferred to work in more accessible communities, where radio contact was easier to establish and food supplies easier to come by. This suggested that Marcos had only accepted work in Mekranoti because he already knew some Kaiapo—I envied his fluency and the fact that he could joke with the Indians. Also, probably more important, he received an excellent salary of which, of course, he couldn't spend a single penny while in the field. Consequently he was able to lead a dissolute and fairly luxurious life during his rare visits to town. Not too bad for someone who hadn't completed his secondary education! But the price he had to pay for these rare moments of extravagance was high. I felt sorry for him.

After a while, Marcos turned the conversation to the Mekranoti. He'd arrived in the village less than a year before and had only been to the cities twice in the interim. A little over two months before, just prior to my arrival, he'd accompanied the village men to Baú, a smaller Mekranoti village to the north. "The men ought to go there every year to harvest Brazil nuts near the Baú and Pitiatiá rivers," he said, continuing: "A FUNAI boat picks up the nuts and transports them to Belém, where they are sold. The Indians get paid for their work, and this is the only significant money earned by the community. But FUNAI failed to send the necessary supplies and tools in time. So after waiting for a few weeks, the Indians decided to return to their village. Just like that. Maybe it was for the better, because tension had grown in Baú. The small community of 50 people there no longer could provide enough food supplies to the 50 male Mekranoti visitors. Tension also grew when the Mekranoti men started courting the Baú women. I understand why. They had nothing to do there, just hanging around all day. The men at Baú complained, but felt helpless. . . . They explained their fears and anxieties to me, and so I let the Mekranoti men go. I stayed behind a few more days to discuss the matter by radio with my superiors, without the Mekranoti hearing all I had to say. It now seems that things will be settled within a few weeks, when another flight is scheduled to Baú to ship the material and food the Mekranoti men asked for."

As Marcos continued by saying that he'd come all the way on foot, I interrupted his monologue to ask if that plane would also come to our village. "I guess not," he said. "Our plane only comes here two or three times a year. It was here just before you arrived, so we can expect it to return only in February or March." It seemed bizarre to be talking about months when living in a place where no calendars were kept. I didn't know what day of the week it was, let alone the date. According to Marcos, it was January 10. Christmas and New Year were already behind us, and I hadn't thought about them at all. As we talked, I prepared pieces of curassow bird with fried manioc slices to eat. Then Marcos left, wanting to put up his hammock before darkness fell. The welcome cool winds presaged a torrential thunderstorm that night.

A few minutes after Marcos had left, a man with a small red cloth hat and dark vest came through my door. In a cheerful, high voice, he greeted me and asked "Where's the coffee?" This was Kenti. Somehow the chemistry between us was perfect from that very first meeting. He wanted to know who I was, where I'd come from, why I was there, why I was occupying Jean's house—and, above all, what kind of trade goods I'd brought with me. Kenti translated my answers for the few men who were sitting on logs pushed against the walls. Nodding, they fired more questions at me which Kenti patiently translated. When I realized that I was actually talking to the Indians through the intermediary of Kenti, I felt as if the doors to the Garden of Eden had opened to me. Now I could

really start working! It seemed as if all of my worries were over. It was already pouring down rain when Kenti indicated that he was leaving. Turning in the doorway, he said, "Tomorrow we start a feast." Then he vanished into the vast darkness occasionally blanched by lightning.

Whatever the feast was that Kenti had mentioned, I didn't find out anything about it the next two days. I kept trying to find Kenti himself, but he always seemed to be out hunting, fishing, or doing whatever else the men did in the daytime away from the village. I spent as much time as possible there, visiting with people or sitting in the men's house. I noticed that the women were working more intensively than they had before, bringing big loads of manioc roots and corn into the village and preparing huge amounts of flour. Krujêt, still my most faithful visitor, explained that the men were about to leave on a trip into the forest. I was eager to go along, but he insisted that I stay behind. There was far too much danger in the forest, and I was certain to have problems with my feet since I was not used to walking there, especially during the rainy season. Krujêt had this particular way of stressing whatever he was saying by prolonging the word he wanted to emphasize, simultaneously letting his voice rise in tone. When he said "Huuuuuurt!" I knew it would hurt a lot. When he talked about swollen feet, he indicated just how big they'd get. I discussed the matter with Kenti and Marcos, and, since they both confirmed everything Krujêt had said, I decided to stay behind. Two days later, I watched most of the men walk into the jungle, each carrying a gun, a machete, and a basket containing a load of manioc or corn flour. As they left the village, they called their dogs, urging them to follow. I felt quite lonely, once again in a village populated by women, children, and a mere handful of men.

Being a nurse (he'd taken a three-month course organized by FUNAI), Marcos took over the business of medical assistance. In fact, he made it clear that I wasn't authorized to provide such assistance at all and declined with thanks my offer to help out when he was away. Since the Indians continued to come to me, saying that I had better medicines than Marcos, this put me in a difficult position. And since providing medical assistance was as good as a full-time job—I'd learned this the hard way—I saw very little of Marcos. I wasn't entirely displeased, because

when I did see him, he talked for hours. His favorite
—not to say his only—topic appeared to be women.
Unmarried, he enjoyed describing the many roman-
tic episodes of his life in detail. He often repeated
stories he'd already told me, and when he did I
noticed that he added more racy details. Telling
these stories was like daydreaming for Marcos.

I knew that since he was a FUNAI agent, it was
important for me to remain on good terms with
Marcos. So I usually dropped in for a visit in the
afternoon on my way to bathe in the river. He often
joined me there, spending an hour or so enjoying
the water and watching the children playing and
adults chatting and eating sweet potatoes. Marcos
came to my house only once, when, quite haughtily,
he told me that radio contact had verified the fact
that my authorization had been approved by his
superiors in Belém. Behaving like Santa Claus, he
announced officially that I could stay and do whatever I'd come to do. Since I could tell that he
expected me to be extremely grateful, I pretended I
was, thanking him profusely while pouring out yet
another cup of coffee.

Like Marcos, Kenti (it turned out) hadn't gone
into the forest with the men. I was amazed. He
insisted on seeing my luggage and immediately

asked for glass beads, ammunition, and a long list
of other things. Later that day, Krujêt came in with
a similar request. It then dawned on me that I'd
been duped. Both Krujêt and Kenti had maneu-
vered me to stay so that they could have access to
my trade goods before the other men. As far as I
could tell, they'd been backed up by Marcos
because he preferred having a westerner around
—a reason I could understand all too well. Having
resolved to join the men on their next forest trip,
miserable feet or not, I spoke to Kenti and made it
clear that I understood what had happened. He
laughed in acknowledgment, but still tried to per-
suade me to give him some trade goods. I agreed to
do so, but only if he'd help me learn Kaiapo. He
agreed. At least once a day, he dropped by to work
for an hour or so. We started off with short, simple
sentences, later turning to more complicated ones.
I was pleased to see that Kenti was a highly patient
and conscious man. He also had a perfect sense of
humor, so we laughed a lot during and especially
after our working sessions.

Working with Kenti, I felt I made enormous
progress in learning Kaiapo. It soon became clear
that there were many instances in which the Mekranoti made differentiations where no such distinc-

43

tions were made in European languages, and vice versa. One of the striking examples was the verb "to eat." An essential difference is expressed in Kaiapo between eating something soft or something hard, eating something you have to chew or that melts in your mouth. Of course, European languages also make a distinction between chewing and eating, but eating among the Mekranoti really only means eating something like manioc or meat. Many other things are not "eaten"; another verb has to used, and using the wrong one might cause you to say something like "I'm eating my drink." Also, the Mekranoti distinguish between only four basic colors: white, red, black, and green/yellow/light blue. Variations can be indicated either by referring to something in the environment or by adding an adjective, as in "dark red" or "light red." In this way too, a distinction can be made between "black" (referring to black as well as dark blue) and "really black" (explicitly meaning black).

I also discovered that counting was of no real importance in Mekranoti society. This indifference is reflected in Kaiapo vocabulary, making it difficult to count above six. For higher numbers or larger amounts, people will say "as many as there are trees in a forest" or "as many as I have fingers and toes." Etiquette was also apparent in the language. The Mekranoti never say "Thank you," because the receiving of gifts is taken for granted: either you're receiving something in return for something you've already given, or the giver expects to get something in return. In a society where reciprocity is a basic rule, there's no need to thank anybody. I often had difficulty not being able to thank someone who'd been friendly or helpful; the closest I could get was to say "That's all right." Also, one never said "Good morning," "How are you?" or "Good-bye." If I met someone on a path, I just asked "Where are you going?"—often not waiting for an answer. When people parted, they just said "I'm leaving," regardless of how long they were leaving for.

I also learned that Kaiapo contained more personal pronouns than I was accustomed to. The Mekranoti distinguish between "I," "you [singular] and I," "you [plural including you] and I," "we [small group including you] and I," "we [small group excluding you] and I," and so on But probably the most difficult challenge involve expressing units of time. To indicate whether som hing had

happened yesterday, a few weeks ago, or a long time ago often proved extremely complex and laborious—somehow I knew I'd have a hard time working on the group's history! Also, differentiation was made depending on whether the person telling a story had been present at the events being described or not. I had my hands full trying to see clearly in this linguistic labyrinth, and in the end I was glad that, due to the departure of the men, I wasn't being bothered constantly by people asking for medicines, knives, or whatever else they could think of.

With the men gone, I thought the occasion might be appropriate for taking my first pictures. Although I always had my camera around, I hadn't taken a single picture in the two months I'd been in Mekranoti. Believing as always that it would be best to proceed slowly, I decided to start with Polaroids and only to take pictures of people with particularly nice body paintings. My first subject, Kôkôba, a girl of about 12, was quite nervous when I mimicked that I wanted to take her picture. People standing around us urged her to allow me to proceed, so she finally posed for me. Then I faked taking a picture with my normal camera—with no film in it—just so that people would get used to me handling it in front of them. After a few minutes, I gave Kôkôba the developed Polaroid picture, and everyone admired the result. Although they'd seen photographs before, the Mekranoti had never experienced the miracle of instant pictures. It met with the success

The author in 1974 when he had his head shaved and his eyebrows removed.

Nokàti carrying fire wood, with her son in a woven sling.

I'd hoped for. Several women asked me to take pictures of their children, whom they'd adorned with fresh paint, necklaces, armlets, and so on. I soon ran out of Polaroid film and gestured that I could only use the other camera as a result. So I started taking pictures, real pictures, first of Marcos, then of Indians posing, and finally of candid subjects.

A few days after the men had left, a man who'd stayed behind had his head shaved with a razor blade by his wife. The part that was shaved was that between his forehead and a point on the crown of his head. This special hairstyle, called *jôkàr* (shaved hair on top of the head), is typical of the Kaiapo. It was explained to me that this haircut warded off the spirits of the dead, which were particularly feared when a major dance was to be held. Such spirits are said to be attracted by singing and thus might endanger the dancers. The lighter, "whitish" tops of adolescent and adult dancers' heads are therefore meant to deflect spirits.

The woman who shaved her husband's head on this occasion told me that all of the men would be having their heads shaved for the big dance that was coming up soon. She insisted that I too have my head shaven. Although I refused politely, over the next couple of days nearly all the women insisted that I have my head shaved and my body painted. I kept refusing. I had no intention at all of "going native." In the end, however, I gave in. Pleased, Nokàti (Nokàjabjê's sister) shaved my head, scraping harshly bit by bit, without using any soap. She did her job quickly but efficiently; no blood was spilled. The many people watching us laughed, and I felt uneasy about the whole thing. It took a few minutes before I dared to look at myself in the mirror. And when I did, I was shocked: I was unrecognizable; my entire face looked different, older. I then realized I had to shave off my beard as well. This I did myself. The women were pleased, since a full body painting required painting on the cheeks. When they insisted that I remove my eyebrows and eyelashes, however, I put my foot down, fearing that they wouldn't grow back.

Nokàti painted me in her house. She first chewed some genipap pulp together with the pits and then mixed these in a half-gourd with charcoal and a little water and saliva. Using a fine, flexible palm-rib stylus, she meticulously applied the motifs line by line to my body and face. When I asked whether I should remove my shorts just as the Mekranoti men did on such occasions, she indicated that it wasn't necessary. It soon became obvious that she was applying a painting that, unlike normal ones, didn't cover my entire body. Instead, it consisted of four separate blocks, leaving my waist area unpainted. This was the type of painting usually applied to dance leaders. The painting took more than two hours to complete. I was itching all over. Not only did the paint tickle but I also was covered with mosquito bites. Since I'd been forced to lie still for so long, the small daytime mosquitoes had taken advantage of the situation to attack me ferociously. Nokàti saw that I was suffering and frequently interrupted her work to try to chase the blood-suckers away. When I finally stood up, she and the other women seemed pleased with the result. I was fortunate that she'd painted me because, as I found out later, she was one of the most skilled women in this regard. Everyone said that I now looked "like a Mekranoti." What pleased them the most was the fact that I'd agreed to have my head shaved. As a result, I was given my first indigenous name, Jôkàr.

Oxidation occurs when genipap dye comes into contact with the skin. I wasn't allowed to bathe that day. When I awoke the next morning, my hammock, blanket, T-shirt, and shorts were entirely blackened by paint. I hurried to the river to bathe. The topmost layer of paint, composed primarily of charcoal, disappeared. I thought that the painting had been unsuccessful because I could hardly see it on my body anymore. But soon, dark blue, nearly black drawings became apparent. Depending on the quantity of water and saliva added, and on the age of the genipap fruit, the paint remains visible on the skin for eight to fourteen days, and it is simply impossible to wash or rub away. I was proud of my painting and was pleased to see that the Indians were, too.

Twelve days after the men had left, I heard the women wailing. Grabbing my camera, I ran into the village. The men were entering the plaza in single file, many of them carrying forest tortoise or packets of meat on their back. I took some pictures: my first real action shots. Some of the men looked annoyed, but most of them didn't seem to mind. When they all had gathered in front of the men's house, a young leader moved to the front of the group and delivered a short ritual address. Then everyone dispersed.

The next day, the women got up early. Three big fires were lit in the plaza to heat stones. The meat the men had brought was being trimmed, and slices of it were being wrapped together with manioc or corn flour in banana leaves. These packets were put between the heated stones, and the "oven" was then covered with sand and more banana leaves. Watching this scene with interest, I was unaware that I was missing the more important activity occurring inside the houses, where the other women were painting their husbands and shaving their heads. All sorts of ornaments were being made and put on. That afternoon, as I was sitting in the men's house with a few of the boys, we suddenly heard singing. A long line of decorated men emerged from the eastern side of the plaza, holding their hands behind their heads. In this pose, they were meant to symbolize flying birds, which occupy an important place in Mekranoti mythology. A few women participated, carrying the small children that were being honored during this festival, which, I'd found out, was the *panh-te* naming ceremony in

which the ritual names of some of the children were being confirmed.

The row of dancers was led by Kamkra (the man I'd nicknamed Al Capone), the chief's oldest son, who wore a revolver in a holster fashioned from a husk. Several of the other men wore socks, shoes or boots, hats, or sunglasses. It was as if they were showing off their wealth. The dance having taken less than half an hour, all of the men entered the men's house except for the two dance leaders, Kamkra and Tàkàkmê (a senior man with a small wooden lip disk), who remained in the plaza. A few other men and women then took their places in front of the two dance leaders, together with the children being honored. Kamkra and Tàkàkmê sang a few verses to each child, as if to bless them. When both men had moved back toward the men's house, a young man nearby said to me "Arỳp ket" (It's finished). This *panh-te* was the smallest naming ceremony I witnessed; others took months and involved a lot of singing and many different dances.

The day after the ceremony, in the early afternoon, people all over the village started shouting. Everyone dropped what they were doing and started running, either to their house to put on some clothing or toward the landing strip. "Mànkà!" (Airplane), they yelled. It was only as I ran toward the landing strip that I heard the sound of the plane. How could the Indians have heard it so long before I had? I was extremely excited. I heard the Indians speculating about who might be

Irega, one of the most cheerful and most stubborn women in the village, preparing manioc flour.

During the final dance of the *panh-te* naming ceremony, the beautifully adorned honored children are carried by their ritual friends.

coming: Jean? FUNAI? As we stood waiting, I saw that most of the adults—especially the women—were dressed in western clothes. Since I hadn't seen so many dresses since the day I arrived, I realized that clothes were often put on for formal occasions like the arrival of a plane. I wasn't sure whether this was done out of modesty or to show off wealth, but guessed that both factors were significant.

Pointing toward the east, some of the Indians started yelling, having sighted the small missionary's plane, which proceeded to land more easily than when I'd flown in. Out climbed Jean, who greeted the Indians, Marcos, and—finally—me. Having asked me how things were going, she didn't wait for my reply, turning instead to talk to the Indians. I went over to greet Mel, who had kindly brought me some bread.

Everyone returned to the village. As Jean entered her house, she realized that I'd been living there and became extremely angry, screaming that I was the most inconsiderate person she'd ever met, that I had no right to install myself in her house, that she hoped I hadn't touched her radio (I didn't even know where it was), and that I had to move out immediately. As Mel left without saying anything to set up Jean's radio antenna, the Indians came to my defense, explaining to Jean that they'd lodged me in her house, that they were sure I hadn't touched her belongings, and that I'd helped them with medicines. Jean, however, didn't want to listen to reason, so I left immediately. Although sev-

eral people offered me places to stay, old Beprôrôk came up with the most interesting offer. Behind his house he had an empty old hut in which he stored rice. If I wanted to, I could stay there. Not knowing how much I'd regret my decision, I accepted his offer.

All of the Indians helped me move into my new "home," which, I soon realized, was the most miserable one in the village. I speculated (correctly, as I later discovered) that it was the last vestige of the village that had been abandoned approximately seven years prior to my arrival. In untraditional fashion, under a series of influences beyond their control, the Mekranoti hadn't moved their village site since the early 1960s, instead building a new village every 10 years or so at a maximum distance of some 200 meters from the previous one. Although the roof on my new abode needed considerable repairs, it was still unquestionably the very best part of the house. The walls of wooden planks were barely standing; so many were missing that it seemed as if the house had several doors, and many of the planks were quite rotten. The floor consisted not of hardened clay, as it did in all of the other houses, but of loose sand in which insects thrived. I soon found out that these included fleas and jiggers. A few days after my move, I began to feel intense itching around some of my toenails and on the soles of my feet. At first I didn't mind, but as time passed, the itching became agonizing, and I started having difficulty walking. When I took a close look at my feet, I discovered strange-looking light-colored circles between three and six millimeters in diameter and with a small black dot at the center of each circle. Unaware of what I was dealing with, I decided to remove these "pests" with a needle and a knife, a miserable operation in the process of which I managed to remove quantities of my own flesh, somewhat reducing my mobility for a while. I then bathed the wounds in alcohol. The operation was extremely painful, but at least I'd stopped the intense itching. Later on, I found that extreme pain was a successful means of annihilating intense itching. The Mekranoti clearly knew this: I once observed a man knocking his son's head against a bench, and when I asked what on earth he was doing, he replied that the child could cope better with a bearable headache than with an unbearable toothache.

By the time I found out that I was dealing with jiggers—burrowing parasites that lay eggs in living flesh until the whole foot is eaten away—I'd discovered an easier method of dealing with them. Asking me for a needle or safety pin, one of the Mekranoti boys patiently removed the parasites without bursting their egg sacs. The trick was to remove the parasite eggs and all. If the sac broke, the parasite often remained, boring deeper and deeper into my foot. There were periods when they made me particularly crazy.

During the first few days in my new home, I was especially bothered by chickens, who did their very best to chase me away, jumping up and defecating on each and every one of my bags, parcels, papers, and cooking utensils and persistently churning up the "floor" (which probably had been hard before they arrived) so that the room was filled with dust. I feared for my cameras. These new neighbors of mine in no time managed to dismantle one of the illusions I had as a city boy, to wit that roosters only crow in the early morning. I'll never forget the first night in my new home. At about midnight, a rooster started crowing less than half a meter from my right ear. Jumping up, I scared the creature away, but revenge soon followed when, about two hours later, the monster charged again. I hardly slept. Things got worse when at about 4:00 a.m. I felt something crawling on my chest. I never moved so quickly in my entire life. Leaping out of my hammock, I switched on my flashlight just in time to see the culprit: a rat that had entered my hammock by running down the cords. Suddenly aware of many night sounds, I looked around and spotted hundreds of big brownish spiders on the walls and on my luggage. I'd seen some of these spiders in Jean's house, but here there were many, many more. And although I wasn't particularly afraid of spiders—or of any other creature, for that matter—I knew that a bite from one of these spiders would really hurt. Some of the Indians kept small monkeys in their houses specifically to hunt them. To make things worse, I discovered a crowd of rats enjoying the rice stored on the platform. Crawling back into my hammock, I knew I wouldn't be able to close my eyes for one single minute.

Next morning, the first thing I did was to hang my mosquito net around my hammock. During the preceding weeks, I'd often regretted having brought it, since it seemed a cumbersome, useless thing. But now I was thrilled to have it. At least I'd be able to

sleep at night, knowing that I'd be safe from nocturnal visitors. This turned out to be a sensible decision, because no more than two nights later, I was awakened by the agonizing shriek of a rat being devoured by a snake on the platform.

Since I had no table, benches, or platforms on which to store my possessions, I simply placed them on some planks. A big wooden block served as a seat, and I did all my cooking on the kerosene fire, another cumbersome item I was glad to have brought. I regretted not having any plastic or ceramic plates, though, because eating hot food from a metal plate without anything to rest it on isn't particularly pleasant.

I noticed that, as soon as I'd moved into my new house, the number of people who dropped in for a visit decreased. Was this because, with Jean's arrival, potential visitors now had the choice of three different hosts to distract them? Or was it because I had the least luxurious accommodation? In a way, the decrease in visitors didn't bother me, since it gave me more time to work on my notes. On the other hand, if people were loosing interest in me, it would make research difficult in the long term.

On the third day after my move, Krujêt didn't show up at all. Neither did Ngreti, one of Beprôrôk's sons, who'd become one of my most faithful visitors. I felt very much at ease with him because he considerately corrected my pronunciation. With his large and expressive mouth, Ngreti was a perfect teacher in that regard. As we got to

After the dance, the ritual leaders perform a blessing song for the well-being of the honored children.

48

know each other better, I started working with him on the group's complex history, ethnohistory being one of my main research topics. When he too failed to show up, I decided to go to Marcos's place. Pleased to see me, Marcos didn't stop talking. He had only one other visitor and didn't seem to mind my being there at all. When I inquired about the situation, he explained that there were those among the Mekranoti who preferred to have closer contacts with FUNAI and those who preferred to be closer to the missionaries. As he talked, I was reminded of my first view of the village from the air, with the almost perfect circular layout of the houses. The FUNAI house was located to the west, that of the mission to the east. It occurred to me that this diametrical opposition symbolized the opposition between two different approaches to the Indians and that in the end, the Indians themselves would fall victim to it. My own house, located to the south, added a third pole of attraction. I became determined to deal with this situation as neutrally as possible, maintaining balanced relationships with the different westerners involved as well as with the community as a whole.

Crossing the village on my way home that evening, I made a brief stop at the men's house. It was then that I understood the immediate reason for the sudden drop in visitors. Since the entire village population had reunited after a long separation, normal life had resumed in all of its dimensions. The men's house was alive with talk and laughter, and there was a lot of running to and fro the houses. In the distance I could discern the women sitting in front of the houses, with the children playing around them. The men were pleased with my nocturnal visit. Beprôrôk stood up and walked around the men's house, giving his evening speech. Although I still couldn't understand much of what he was saying, I could tell that he was speaking about another naming ceremony.

When I asked Kenti about the ceremony the next day, he seemed amazed that I hadn't heard about the dance the men were to perform that same afternoon. The whole day was spent in preparations. Men were painted by female relatives, others made or repaired feather headdresses, and still others passed the time in the men's house chatting excitedly. At about 4:00 p.m., the dancing finally started. The men, nearly all carrying guns on their left shoulders, stood one next to the other in a half-circle and began to sing. After a few minutes, a group of women joined in, dancing behind the men. As I watched, taking a few pictures and making notes, Jean walked up. I hadn't really seen her since her arrival, probably because we'd been trying to avoid one another. She stood at a certain distance from me, but I noticed that she occasionally looked my way. Gathering my courage, I went over to her. We were both quite uncomfortable to begin with, and I sensed that she regretted her previous behavior, even though she was too proud to admit it. In order to avoid discussing the scene she'd made, we talked about the dance, which Jean seemed to think was being performed to thank me for the medical help I'd given the Indians.

Jean invited me to have a meal with her that evening. Although she welcomed me cordially, and we talked for a long time, I barely paid attention. In my mind I kept trying to discover the real reason for the beautiful dance the Indians had performed. I'd seen this dance before in Gorotíre, where the Indians had performed it when a photographer asked people to dance so that he could take pictures. I'd also seen it in documentary films and in pictures published in magazines. There was no doubt that it was the most frequently performed Kaiapo dance. Sitting in Jean's house, I thought perhaps the Indians had danced to show Jean that they liked me and that I wasn't such a bad guy after all. I'd been warned by colleagues that the Indians hated antagonism between westerners living in their communities, in extreme cases severing contact with the feuding parties. If in fact this had been the Mekranoti's main motive, their diplomacy worked perfectly, because it did lead to rapprochement between Jean and myself, a rapprochement that later became a real friendship.

Jean told me that she'd heard that the next day an important naming ceremony was to start. The next morning, Kenti confirmed what Jean had said, adding that the men wouldn't be leaving on a forest migration right now because this was to be a major ceremony requiring several weeks of preparation. I was delighted, not only because of the ceremony, but also because the men wouldn't be leaving right away. I asked Kenti if he could find me someone who could make me a table, two benches, and a few platforms, and he said he would arrange it. The negotiations as to who would participate in the work and how I would pay them took exactly two weeks. It took another 10 days before the work actually started.

The *tàkàk* naming ceremony was much more elaborate than the simple *panh-te* one I'd already witnessed. Naming is the most frequently recurring theme in the more elaborate Mekranoti ceremonies, which are commonly referred to by the term *mere-remex* (the people who show off beautifully). During major ceremonies, most ritual performances were given in the central plaza. This actually involved a reversal of ordinary social space, since the village center, normally devoted to activities based on friendship (i.e. non-kinship), became the domain of activities dominated by family ties. The beauty to which the term *mereremex* refers is not only visual but also arises from group activity, i.e. the joint effort required to "socialize" the names of persons and precious objects. Personal names are taken from nature by shamans who contact nature spirits and learn new names and songs from them. Since these names derive from nature, they have to be socialized. This is the function of the major naming ceremonies.

The Mekranoti make a distinction between two categories of personal names: "ordinary" names and "great" names. The sources for ordinary names are legion; they can refer to things in the environment, parts of the body, personal experiences, and so on. Each great name has two parts: a ceremonial prefix and a simple suffix. There are eight ceremonial prefixes, which are untranslatable. Except for one, each of these prefixes has its own naming ritual in which names with only that prefix can be confirmed. There are also four other naming ceremonies during which names of any prefix can be confirmed. A few days after birth, a child is given a number of ordinary and great names; in this way, some people receive more than 30 names. While both an ordinary and a great name can be used as a forename, it is considered more appropriate to have a great name confirmed in a ceremony at a later date. Confirmation takes place only after a child has acquired elementary motor and language skills, in other words between the ages of two and eight.

Since each person receives great names based on different ceremonial prefixes, each child should therefore in theory be honored in more than one naming ceremony. This is seldom the case in practice, however, due to the considerable means required by the parents, who act as the sponsors of naming ceremonies and who must provide daily

During the daily dances of the *tàkàk* naming ceremony, the honored children are taken by their ritual friends to the village plaza. Although these children and their friends are beautifully adorned, some wear western clothes as protection against mosquitoes.

nourishment for the singers and dancers. As these ceremonies can go on for months, enormous quantities of food must be obtained and prepared. Parents can turn to relatives for support in this great task, but not everyone is willing—or able—to bear such a heavy economic burden.

Each of the 11 different naming ceremonies consists of a long series of dances, chants, and ritual performances unique to it. Between two and five children are honored during each naming ceremony. The Mekranoti term for children honored during a naming ceremony is *mereremex*, the same term used to refer to major ceremonies in general. Each child is assisted by two or more unrelated ritual friends of both sexes whose task it is to help him or her in all the difficult phases of life. Naming is one of the most important occasions during which the help of ritual friends is solicited.

I enjoyed every minute of the *tàkàk* naming ceremony. Now that I was able to communicate a little, I felt I'd finally begun to work. In connection with the ceremony, a large number of utensils and ornaments were brought out that I hadn't seen before. Material culture was another research topic, and the interest I showed provided a real breakthrough in my relationship with the men. Apparently, I was the first westerner to evidence any interest at all in the things they made and how they made them. In addition, I was interested not only in elaborate feather headdresses but also in more mundane things—baskets, mats, pipes, whatever the Mekranoti made.

During and following the *tàkàk* naming ceremony, both the men and the women started showing me their artifacts and tools whenever I visited their homes. As soon as I'd toured the village a few times in this way, I thought it was time to start collecting the ethnographic items I'd promised to museums in Antwerp and Geneva. As had been the case with the medical treatments two months before, trading was of major importance in becoming closer to the men and proved of immense help in learning the language. Though I relied on Kenti during the first transactions, after a few days I began to do them on my own. This forced me to make appointments, discuss manufacturing processes, ask questions about makers and users, learn about family ties and ritual functions, and so on. Of course, things didn't always go as planned. One day, I'd made an appointment with Ngreti to see a basket he'd recently made and wanted to trade. Our appointment was set by pointing to the position the sun would be in. However, when I arrived at Ngreti's house, he was making love to his wife. Although I was embarrassed, he didn't seem to mind and merely asked me to return a little later.

In the meantime, the *tàkàk* naming ceremony continued. Each morning, just before sunrise, the men gathered in front of the men's house. Standing in two groups (these corresponded to the two men's societies that existed at the time), they sang. The idea was that the singing would take no more than an hour and that it should continue until the sun had risen. So the trick was to start a little after 5:00 a.m. One group would begin, and just before they ended their verse, the other group would start singing another verse, and so on. All went well until one rainy day when the men started singing well before 4:00 a.m. I assumed that this was intentional, that on this occasion another activity had to take place between the singing and sunrise. After about half an hour or so, one of the men came and asked me to check my "flat circlet" (wristwatch) to see if the sun was about to rise. When I explained that it was still much too early, the men were upset and disappointed. Due to the heavy clouds, they'd been unable to see the moon or stars and thus had miscalculated the time. Attempts were made to assign blame for this unfortunate mistake, and a discussion ensued as to whether the singing should continue or whether it could be interrupted to start again at a later time. The elder men won the argument, and the singing continued. It was also decided that from then on, they'd wake me to check the time before they began to sing.

These early morning songs were followed by a brief warlike dance in which all of the men wore traditional weapons (bows and arrows, or clubs) and danced in two groups, symbolically opposing the two men's societies. Following this dance, there were daily races between pairs of men or boys. Everyone would line up at one side of the plaza, and a senior man would choose pairs of men or boys of about the same age. Then, assisted by onlookers, he'd give a yell and push the runners as a sign that the race should begin. Nobody ever kept track of the winners: that didn't seem to be of any immediate importance. The essential point was to improve agility. For the younger men, however, this was also an opportunity to impress the female spectators. So the men and boys ran as fast as they could across the plaza. This was always a happy time. I was often asked to run against an adolescent or a young man. One day, I tripped and fell flat on my face. General hilarity ensued. One old woman simply went to pieces, and I was afraid she might choke. I became the main subject of many jokes in the days that followed (and the event is recalled whenever I return to the village, even today, 20 years later). Much to my embarrassment, news of the incident was transmitted to other villages, so that whenever I visited those communities, I'd be asked to describe the scene over and over again.

The men also gathered every late afternoon in front of the men's house to dance for about half an hour. Although my knowledge of the language was far too limited to permit me to grasp the meaning of the songs they sang—words were often changed when used in songs, making sung Kaiapo into a sort of second language—I noticed that verses changed as the ceremony proceeded. One evening, I saw how this happened. A few men were discussing the songs in the men's house. Old Wajanga seemed to be leading the conversation. He sang a verse I hadn't heard before over and over again, so that everyone present could memorize it. By the next day, the new verse had already been incorporated into the songs. When I asked Kenti to explain, he told me that Wajanga was a shaman who'd been in contact with a monkey that had given him the new verse. It seemed that new songs emerged whenever a naming ceremony was held. The result was that no two ceremonies were alike.

When I noticed that the women were starting to prepare huge amounts of manioc and corn flour again, I thought they were preparing for another forest trek. I'd promised myself that this time I'd go along and was thrilled when I learned that the whole village population would be going, not just the men. When I showed my interest in participating, people reacted enthusiastically at first, but a discussion followed in the men's house. Beprôrôk, Ngreti, Wajanga, and Pingri (Kenti's father-in-law) seemed to do most of the talking. When I sat down next to Kenti and asked him what was going on, he smiled and said that they were discussing my adoption. Although I felt honored, I didn't see why the discussion was so vehement. It went on and on. Finally, when Kenti got up, I followed his example and left the men's house. Kenti told me that they'd continue talking later that evening. When I asked him why the matter was being discussed, he explained that different families wished to adopt me, so they were trying to find out which family I had the most affinity with. I felt somewhat embarrassed. The more Kenti and I talked, however, the better I understood what the men's discussion was really about. I had already noticed that many of the men, both young and old, called me "Kamy" (Brother), and that this expression of affection was often followed by a request for one or another trade good. Since Mekranoti brothers share all they possess, they called me Brother for no other reason than to obtain trade goods without having to give me something in return. The rule of reciprocity worked differently between siblings. Later on, I repeatedly saw westerners arrive in Mekranoti or other Indian villages and assume they'd been adopted immediately when they heard themselves called Brother. However, this was nothing more than a clever way to get trade goods as cheaply as possible. The adoption discussion wasn't about who'd be my siblings, but about who'd be my parents, aunts, and uncles. While these roles might also entail some movement of goods, parents, aunts, and uncles give more than they get in return. While Mekranoti parents provide everything necessary for a child's biological well-being, uncles, aunts, and grandparents provide logistic support and transmit knowledge and the privilege to perform ritual functions or to wear certain ornaments. When I understood this, I felt more flattered than embarrassed.

Later that evening, Kamkra came into my house, addressing me as usual as Brother. I didn't pay any attention until he explained that he meant what he said. I could go along on trek with any adult member of his family, and they'd take care of me, building my shelter and providing me with food. The next morning, Beprôrôk came over for a cup of coffee. Sitting down on one of my cardboard boxes, he called me his son, just like that. From then on, Beprôrôk was my most regular visitor at this early hour, bringing along a huge cup and taking coffee to his house for his kinsmen to drink. Aside from these morning visits, the old chief came infrequently to my house, thus becoming one of the people who asked for gifts sporadically.

It was only when Beprôrôk had left that I realized I'd found my place in the Mekranoti community. I was the son of Beprôrôk and his wife, Ronkà, the brother of Ngreti, Kamkra, Ireteti, and two other men. I also had four adult sisters (among them Nokàjabjê and Nokàti) and a considerable number of sons, daughters, nephews, and nieces. I was on top of the world. My good mood didn't last for long, though. Two days later, a radio message arrived from FUNAI saying that a plane would bring to Baú all the tools, food, and ammunition the Indians had requested, provided that the men returned there immediately to harvest Brazil nuts. Some of the men, especially the younger ones, seemed excited; others, mainly the older ones, were visibly upset, because this meant that the naming ceremony had to be interrupted. The decision was made to go, and so the flour prepared by the women was taken along by the men on their long trip to Baú.

Once the excitement engendered by the ceremony and the men's presence in the village had dissipated, I felt depressed. Life became very monotonous, and I began to feel that I could die for a cold beer. I started dreaming of clean clothes, showers, different food, listening to music, going to the movies. I was suddenly bothered by the lack of choice. In the rain forest, you eat what's there, and there's no way of saying that you'd like to go to a movie. I felt it was time for me to get away to the city and started looking for an excuse to escape. As if guided by telepathy, Jean announced a few days

later that the missionary plane had a flight scheduled to the Kubenkrankênh village the next day. She was willing to ask Mel to come all the way to Mekranoti to pick me up provided that I'd pay for the two extra hours of flying time. She also said that she'd put in a good word for me so that I could fly at a special missionary rate of a hundred dollars, a quarter of the usual rate. I was delighted with her proposal and started packing immediately.

The news got around very quickly. While I was packing, many of the Indians came to ask for trade goods. When I explained I had none left, they asked for my pots and pans, hammock, mosquito net, blanket, sandals, soap—almost everything I had with me. I distributed as much as I could, keeping only the essential items. My sleeping gear was to remain in my house until the plane arrived; one never knew when Mel might have to change plans. Marcos also came by. Although he didn't ask for anything, I saw him eyeing the small amounts of tobacco and coffee I had left. I handed them over, and he seemed pleased. My few remaining batteries went to Jean for her tape recorder. As a result of this unexpected distribution of my belongings, I only had my notes, technical equipment, films, and a few essential clothes to pack. And, of course, the ethnographic material, which I somehow managed to pack in five boxes and a tube for bows, arrows, and clubs.

Mel arrived on schedule. We all stood on the landing strip while he loaded my luggage onto his plane. He didn't seem too pleased with the long tube of Mekranoti weapons, but refrained from comment. I couldn't figure out what he thought of me. While he spoke with Jean, I said good-bye to the Indians, who kept asking when I would be back. I said as soon as possible. Shaking hands with Marcos and Jean, I boarded the plane. Just before we took off, I reminded Jean to contact me as soon as the men returned from Baú. There was no way I was going to miss the remainder of the interrupted *tàkàk* naming ceremony.

A feeling of melancholy came over me as we flew over the village and the surrounding rain forest. I'd spent about three months there and had come to love the Mekranoti, with some of whom I'd begun life-long friendships. The terrible, continuous buzz of the engine bothered me, reminding me that I was no longer accustomed to the sounds of the west. As I watched the seemingly endless panorama of varied shades of green that moved slowly below us, Mel told me that we'd be landing at Gorotíre to pick up Iracema, who had to go to Belém. He also said that if I wanted to return to Mekranoti, he'd take me at the special missionary rate.

Two hours later, we spotted the village of Gorotíre and landed without incident. As soon as I left the plane, I sensed how different it was from Mekranoti. Only a handful of people had come to the landing strip: apparently, planes landed here so often that they no longer inspired much curiosity. The profusion of western clothing, scarcity of body paintings, western hairstyles of most of the younger people, and knowledge of Portuguese among many of the younger men were striking. A few months ago, when I'd arrived in Gorotíre for the first time, I'd enjoyed being there. Now I felt disillusioned. The Indians commented on my body painting, asked who'd applied it and who'd shaved my hair, inquired about people they knew, and seemed to appreciate the fact that I could speak some Kaiapo. They also seemed to look down on the Mekranoti, who "still lived like the ancestors . . . [and] still killed people and walked naked."

Taking Iracema on board, we flew on to Conceição do Araguaia, where Mel left us. Iracema and I took a taxi to the bus station, where we caught a bus to Miracema do Norte, a small town on the main Brasilia–Belém road. There we separated, Iracema heading north while I headed south. My bus was late and I had to wait for nearly four hours in the burning sun. When the bus arrived, the driver wasn't too eager to pick me up. I soon realized that he was staggered by the big "tattoos" I had on my arms and cheeks. When I explained what they were, he smiled, saying I was a fool to live among "savages." While at first he'd insisted that there wasn't enough space to stow all of my gear, especially the bows and arrows, he now felt sorry for me. Removing one of the spare tires, he loaded my things and off we went.

The next day we arrived in Brasilia. As I was completely broke, I went to the Belgian Embassy not only to inform them that I was alive and well but also to see if someone could lend me the money (less than eighty dollars) to get to São Paulo. No one seemed ready to hand over money to an indecent, savage-looking compatriot. However, the affable cultural attaché, whom I'd met before, took pity on me and offered to drive me to a place near the highway to São Paulo. From there I was sure to be able to hitch a ride on one of the many trucks. He even gave me a big sign with "São Paulo" written on it.

Yet no-one stopped to pick me up. When I realized that I was accomplishing nothing by standing on the highway, I crossed the road and, abandoning the sign, just stuck out my thumb. Soon a truck stopped, and I was offered a free ride back to town. The driver was generous enough to take me to the exact address I wanted: a big apartment building where I'd rented rooms some months before. Luckily, the old concierge, Antônia, recognized me. She proposed that I spend the night and said she'd lend me enough money to get to São Paulo.

It's impossible to describe my pleasure at being able to take a shower and use a decent toilet. Yet, while I enjoyed my first night in "civilization," I couldn't shake my melancholy mood. I missed the Mekranoti. I missed their cheerfulness. I missed the smell of genipap and annatto. And I missed the silence. Colleagues had warned me about culture shock, which was normal when arriving in the field. I had it the other way around. I wanted to be left alone. Antônia, seeming to understand what I was feeling, brought me a nice evening meal, handed me the money I needed, and wished me luck.

Arriving in São Paulo, I was received by my good friends Jacques and Maureen, who'd looked after me during my lengthy stays there before I'd been able to join the Mekranoti. This time, they helped me find the necessary money to continue my research. I sold one of my cameras with two lenses. I also decided to sell a number of roles of slide film (at the time extremely expensive in Brazil), as well as a pair of boots I'd never worn. My family also sent some cash. I envied some American anthropologists I'd met in Brazil whose field research was funded by grants. As a Belgian studying in Paris, I was ineligible for grants and so had to finance my trip myself.

After about three weeks, I'd gathered enough money to start purchasing the trade goods and food I needed to return to Mekranoti. As before, I'd be left with only the tiniest reserve when the time came to return to São Paulo from the forest. Once again, I didn't really care. I was all set to return to Mekranoti, and that was all that mattered.

Kenti, the only Mekranoti man who was able to speak Portuguese. Kenti had been an orphan when government agents had contacted the Mekranoti group he lived with during the late 1950s. Fascinated by the agents, he spent a few years with them as they searched for other Mekranoti groups roaming freely in the immense central Brazilian tropical rain forest. Kenti thus learned Portuguese and established himself as the essential go-between whenever foreigners visited his people. During rituals, Kenti would be painted and wear ornaments, but at other times, he preferred to wear a vest and, above all, one or another type of hat.

Beprôrôk wearing his white feathered hat. He'd stolen his Winchester rifle from some Brazilians during a raid sometime in the late 1930s. Born around the turn of the century, he's the oldest Kaiapo chief alive—and probably also the one who clings to tradition the most tenaciously.

Traditionally, when an adolescent girl starts courting, her mother would insist that her boyfriend weave a mat or bag out of burity palm fibers. If the young man couldn't master this weaving technique, he'd stay away from his girlfriend until he'd acquired the necessary skills. Once he did master the technique, he'd finish the artifact using cotton from his girlfriend's red sash or cotton leg bands to make string pendants to adorn it. The bag or mat was then given to the girl, who in turn often gave it to her mother. Good weavers are highly appreciated sons-in-law, since they're capable of providing high-quality mats and baskets. Particularly skilled weavers therefore take great pride in their skills, showing off in the men's house and insisting that others be attentive to their work. Môpti is one of the most talented weavers, spending many hours making mats, baskets, slings, and supports for headdresses.

Akranhi, also a renowned weaver, is a southern Mekranoti man who'd moved to the central Mekranoti community in 1979, preferring its atmosphere of peace and tranquility to the serious fights that had broken out in his own village.

The men's house, one of the most animated sites in the Mekranoti village, is rarely empty. In the early morning or late afternoon, it's the meeting place where important speeches are given by elders or chiefs and where communal activities as well as politics are discussed. During the day, the men's house may serve as the place where handicrafts are manufactured; at night, unmarried men, as well as some married men with pregnant wives or newborn children, sleep there. During periods of ritual performance, the men's house is alive with activity.

Young Ngrano preparing red annatto dye in the men's house and applying it to a friend's face. The red pigment is prepared from seeds from the annatto shrub. Annatto seeds are held together in a shell by a sticky red substance. To store them, they're laid out to dry in the sun and then kept in a gourd with a braided cover or bag of braided palm fibers. When someone wants to use them, the seeds are mixed with water or, better yet, a little palm oil. Annatto dye is usually applied to the forehead and feet, whereas black paint is applied to the body and cheeks. The dye is very volatile and disappears during bathing. It's also often applied to newly made objects such as pipes, ear plugs, and clubs.

63

Of all Mekranoti body painting styles, black motifs applied by hand are the most informative. At the birth of a child, for instance, the husband may not sleep with his wife for a period of time, during which he sleeps in the men's house. Once the child is considered strong enough, the mother allows her husband to return. This change in status is announced publicly by painting, shown here being applied by Nhàkngri, Bepkô's wife.

Everyday paintings are usually applied by the men and adolescent boys in the men's house, using their hands rather than palm-leaf styluses. Here Bàti, Krujêt's youngest son, paints Kàngrà, a young man of the Kreen Akróre tribe who moved to the Mekranoti village in 1979.

65

Môpti adorning himself for the final dance of the corn
festival. The shaved part of his head be intended to ward
off human sapirits that might be attracted by the beautiful
singing.

for me, neither stopping nor looking behind. As agile as cats, they jumped over or bent under huge fallen trees. Due to the recent heavy rainfall, the path was extremely slippery, and I sometimes had difficulty keeping my balance. When the Indians realized this, they cut me a long wooden stick that did help me keep my balance, but that made it even more difficult to walk through thick bush. Particularly troublesome were the numerous flooded areas we had to wade through, with water coming up to our ankles, knees, or waists.

When we were still pretty close to the village, we encountered Nojabjê. Known to be one of the fiercest Mekranoti warriors, he was an impressive sight. At about 50, he was still extremely agile and strong. Having once worn a lip disk, he'd removed it in the mid-1960s, leaving a big hole in his lower lip. During the *tàkàk* naming ceremony, he'd been one of the sponsors. That day, he'd left the forest camp early in the morning to fetch an additional supply of manioc flour from the village. After he'd explained to my two guides where the last camp had been built, we moved on.

The soles of the Indians' feet were as hard as thick leather; mine were as soft as the skin of a newborn baby. I thought my feet were well protected in socks and tennis shoes, but, after a 10-minute walk, they were already sodden. We often used fallen trees to cross the smaller creeks. At these times, the Indians' pigeon-toed way of walking, probably more efficient than other postures on narrow forest paths, allowed them to hold on to the "bridges" with their toes. With my wet feet in wet shoes, I had a particularly hard time on these "bridges," especially when fast-running water reached above them, making it difficult to maintain a grip. On several occasions, I was afraid that all my equipment would end up in the water. I wondered if I'd been foolish to sell my boots in São Paulo, but then I realized that my perspiring feet would've been miserable inside them. The farther we walked, the more painful each step became.

After a while, I noticed that one man would walk ahead at his own pace, while the other stayed behind with me. When we caught up with the first man resting somewhere, smoking his pipe or eating a banana, the two guides would switch off. As a result, I was the only one out of the three of us who walked the whole time. I was too proud and stubborn to ask if I could rest and, after a while, simply stumbled along like a robot.

The farther we went, the harder it became to see the trails and paths. Now the two guides stayed with me. The man at the front sometimes had to cut his way forward with his machete. Weakened and bent under my rucksack, I got snagged in branches; my shirt was torn, and my face was constantly whipped by twigs released as the man in front of me passed along the trail. Whenever I asked if we were almost at the camp, the men would reply "Soon" or "It's very near now." Since we walked and walked, I wondered whether they'd simply lost their way. In the late afternoon, we met Nojabjê again. He smiled when he saw my sweaty body and reddened face—the Indians rarely perspire, and when they do, it's mostly on their noses. I was embarrassed when I realized that this man, carrying a basket filled with at least 50 kilos of manioc flour, had already caught up with us. When he explained that he'd taken a short cut, I got irritated and wished more experienced guides had been appointed to accompany me. Without interrupting his march, Nojabjê soon vanished into the forest in front of us.

We reached the camp at about 4:00 p.m. First we heard a few dogs barking, then the friendly buzz of children playing and adults chatting. I was exhilarated but also exhausted. People were delighted to see me, welcoming me by asking what trade goods I'd brought along. Jean came to say hello and offered me a few bananas, while the Indians invited me to move into a shelter next to that of my "father," Beprôrôk. In the distance, I heard my two guides bragging that in spite of my uncontrollable perspiration, I had not asked to stop once. This made me feel a bit more dignified. It was clear that by having said I'd return and then having done so, I'd taken what was undoubtedly one of the most important steps in building a close relationship with the Mekranoti.

The first thing I did was to take off my soaking wet socks and shoes and put them over a fire to dry. I had a quick bath in the only running water around, a small muddy creek that barely reached to my knees. The sand at the bottom was slippery and loose, and the Indians showed me how to glide my feet through it so that I'd scare the stingrays away rather than stepping on them. Returning to the

An early morning view of a forest camp including a temporary shelter.

camp, I put on the only fresh clothes I had. Having hung up my hammock and mosquito net, I discovered that I had four major blisters on my feet. By the time I'd settled in, darkness had fallen. I had a quick bite of some of the meat one of my "sisters" had made and soon fell into a deep sleep. A few hours later, however, I was awakened by a heavy wind announcing a tempestuous rainfall. In the darkness, I saw the women strengthening the flimsy shelters, which consisted of nothing more than a few wooden poles and some palm and wild banana leaves. Nokàti came to check mine and suggested that I sleep on the ground, as most of the Indians did, rather than in my hammock, which would get soaked. She fetched some leaves to cover the damp ground and a log to act as a pillow. Having secured my belongings against the rain, I fell asleep again.

A terrifying storm soon hit the camp with heavy winds that bent and broke some of the trees. I heard the Indians saying that a rotten tree somewhere to my left was cracking and would soon fall. It must have been a big tree, because when it fell,

it dragged a few smaller trees with it. On a later occasion, the Indians warned me to move just a few minutes before a falling tree hit our camp. After the winds, the rain came, seemingly from all directions. Soon all of the Indians were awake. They sat in tight clusters, seeking the best protection from the rain. Since there was no way to keep both me and my luggage dry, I left my luggage in the safest spot and squatted down in what I considered to be the second best one. Soon I was soaked. It poured and poured, and the resulting damage could be seen the next morning. Only a few shelters remained intact, while the others had nearly been washed away.

The situation didn't seem to bother anyone, because an hour or so later we all had packed our belongings and were off to a new site. The younger men were sent on ahead to clear the path with their machetes. Then the other men followed, some of them carrying "ladders" of forest tortoise tied in rows between pairs of wooden sticks. Such "ladders" could carry a maximum of fifteen tortoises, be as high as three meters, and weigh up to sixty kilos. Transporting them through the forest was no easy task, and that was why the younger men were sent ahead to clear a passage through the overgrowth. Since it's difficult to store large quantities of meat in tropical rain forests for long periods, meat was eaten in the forest when the Indians were on trek, except for the forest tortoises, which were kept for the final feast. This made sense since tortoise can live for a long time without eating or drinking. The transportation problem was solved by using "ladders."

The last to leave for the new camp were the women and children, who carried baskets filled with manioc flour, bunches of bananas, mats, pets, pots, pans, and much more. The new camp was set up a few kilometers from the previous one. It was amazing to see how quickly the women erected the new shelters. Barely arrived at the new site, they dropped their belongings and disappeared into the forest, soon reappearing with loads of big leaves, wooden poles, and strips of bark. Construction was very well organized; everybody knew exactly what to do and when. Relatives collaborated to make big shelters, and the structure of the main village was copied as closely as possible. My shelter was built next to Beprôrôk's by three of my "sisters." After four forked poles had been stuck in the ground, four horizontal poles were placed across them. Then leaves were placed on top and at the rear, occasionally fastened with bark strips. Building my shelter took less than 15 minutes.

While the women were preparing the shelters and searching for stones to make ovens, the men departed for their daily hunting session. The camp was a very pleasant sight. The children were having a wonderful time. Whereas in the village the playground of the younger ones was restricted to the plaza, here they could run around in the forest, discovering all sorts of reptiles, insects, and birds and trying out their bows and arrows on something other than melons. The sounds of the camp echoed against the wall of trees, creating a pleasant, slightly mysterious ambiance. By noon, the first men had already returned. While still quite far away, they started singing in a high falsetto. The songs reflected the kind of animal they'd hunted, so the women knew who'd killed what. Hunting, which in the distant forest seemed to require less effort than work in the village, occurred only during seasonal or ceremonial treks, and meat seemed pretty easy to get. I had the impression that this made everyone happy and more relaxed. Or maybe this seemed to be the case because everything happened out in the open.

All of the men had returned by early afternoon and had gathered at the center of the camp. Things became very lively, but unfortunately it began to rain. The rain persisted for three entire days. These weren't tormenting tropical rains, but rather continuous soft rains accompanied by a drop in temperature. My clothes were never dry, and I worried about my technical equipment. I was glad I had two pairs of shoes. One pair was always hanging over a fire until both shoes were brown and rigid with smoke. Due to the incessant rains, however, I was never able to keep my shoes dry for more than a few hours.

In the forest, there were fewer small mosquitoes, but their place was taken by innumerable sweat bees that seemed to fancy me. They buzzed around my head, entering my nostrils and mouth and making it difficult for me to see and hear. The Indians seemed to be bothered much less, and I thought this might be because I sweated more than they did. I tried bathing frequently, but the bees attacked me the moment I came out of the water. I thought perhaps they were attracted by my soap and refrained from using any for a while. This made no difference. In the end, I smeared my body with indigenous dyes and my hair with palm oil just as the Indians did. Yet the bees continued to pick me out even when I was sitting in the midst of some 50 men. So I gave up.

There were also mosquitoes of the kind I knew from Europe and of which the anopheles is the most famous because it can carry malaria. These mosquitoes never quit; they were around day and night. I tried several repellents, none of which seemed to have any effect, mostly because my perspiration just washed them away. The only way to cut down the number of bites was either to sit continually in the smoke from the fires or to wear shirts with long sleeves and trousers tucked into my socks. I opted for the second alternative, but this made me perspire more, thus encouraging the sweat bees.

Except for some coffee, I hadn't brought any food, and this proved to be a good decision. Meat

was abundant. The Mekranoti preferred to hunt big game, and we ate tapir, wild pigs, and deer. Such large mammals couldn't be found every day, however, so monkeys, wild fowl, and especially wild tortoise and agoutis (large rodents) were hunted frequently. Birds were usually hunted only for their colorful feathers; jaguars, pumas, and ocelots were killed only if they crossed a hunter's path. Since very little ammunition was available, I saw several men go into the forest with clubs or bows and arrows. In fact, it was in order to get batteries as well as ammunition for their rifles (nearly every man had one, and some had three plus a revolver) that the Mekranoti worked each year harvesting Brazil nuts in Baú. Since they'd asked me to, I'd brought some ammunition along, although as a foreigner, I'd had some difficulty buying it. Some of the administrators I'd dealt with seemed to think I might be arming a guerrilla group.

One day, Kàjkwa came to the camp carrying a big jaguar on his shoulders. It was an impressive animal, and I wondered how he'd been able to kill it without a gun. In fact, he'd simply beaten it over the head with a wooden club. The senior men explained that according to Mekranoti tradition, young men were sent into the forest just before they

got married. Armed only with long, slender clubs, they weren't allowed to return to the village until they'd killed a large mammal. While some were lucky and managed to do this quickly, others stayed alone in the forest for weeks. The Mekranoti believed that eating the meat of wild cats causes some people to become ill. Only young boys ate jaguar meat. Although I was discouraged from doing so, I insisted on tasting it, too. The meat was extremely tough, and I was terribly sick the next day. Luckily enough, due to the ongoing rain, the camp wasn't moved immediately, so I was able to rest. Acclimating to life on trek was difficult for me. The heat and humidity made me pay for everything I did.

One morning, I heard loud, persistent wailing. A woman was sitting with her four-year-old daughter on her lap. The child, who didn't look well, had apparently been stung by a scorpion. Although such bites aren't usually fatal for adults, they can be for children. I hadn't brought anything to use against scorpion bites, so, after consulting with Jean, we applied a Brazilian medicine meant for snakebite or scorpion stings. Unfortunately, the syrup failed in this instance, and that same afternoon the camp was filled with the sudden tragic wailing of the child's mother and a few other women. The next

72

Tàkàkpin, one of my closest companions during forest treks and hunts. He's wearing a highly coveted necklace with jaguar teeth.

day, the parents took the child back to the village to have it buried there.

Each late afternoon, the men gathered in the center of the camp to have their daily chat and to listen to the speeches that senior tribesmen were expected to give occasionally. Not all of the men were especially eloquent, so it was common for them to try out their first speeches in the forest. If they were unable to capture their listeners' attention, they refrained from giving further speeches. Those who were successful continued to speak at gatherings in the village later on. The men also sang every afternoon, rehearsing the songs they'd sing in falsetto during the final days of the *tàkàk* naming ceremony. In the forest, they sang quietly, explaining that the songs shouldn't be sung aloud until they were known well by everyone. There was also another reason. The Mekranoti greatly feared the spirits in the forest and didn't want them to hear their singing, because the spirits would then be attracted to the campsite. This would be dangerous, because people who weren't trained as shamans could die at the mere sight of such a spirit. Ironically, the low-decibel singing in the superb forest setting made the songs sound to me as if they were being produced by spirits.

Men usually hunted alone, setting out one after the other very early in the morning. Those lucky enough to kill something immediately returned around noon. Others who had no luck or who were exploring fresh tracks roamed the woods until the evening. Out of fear of spirits, no-one was eager to spend a night alone in the forest. We were already in our fourth camp when I let it be known that I wanted to join one of the men on a hunt. Boti, a senior man renowned for his hunting skills, said he'd take me along the next morning. Wearing nothing but his penis sheath, he carried a bow and arrows, a machete, and a small bag containing his pipe, tobacco, some ammunition, and a small mirror. I carried nothing and wore a shirt, shorts, socks, and my usual tennis shoes. With Boti leading, we moved quickly. While I had trouble keeping up with my guide, he found time to stop occasionally to listen to the sounds of the forest, identify smells, or peer into the vegetation trying to locate prey. That day, he only managed to catch a single forest tortoise. Since he found it close to the camp, he merely turned it on its back and continued his search for other game. When that failed, we retraced our steps, and Boti tied the tortoise onto his back with bark string. He then began to sing to let the camp know what he was bringing back.

I noticed that the men never came home empty-handed. Even if a man hadn't killed anything, he was sure to bring a few medicinal plants, some wild fruit, or fibers for making utensils and decorations. Arriving back at the campsite, the successful hunter would give his kill to his wife or, if he was single, to his mother or sister. Forest tortoises, on the other hand, were handed to the sponsors of the *tàkàk* naming ceremony, who tied them between the poles on the tortoise "ladders." Each morning, the male sponsors checked to see whether the tortoise were still alive by knocking on their bellies. If the sound was too hollow, the animal was considered dead and was removed. By the end of my second week in the forest, I counted over two hundred tortoises, but the sponsors said this wasn't enough for "a really big ceremony."

Having hunted with Boti, the next day I joined Tàkàkpin, Kamra's oldest son and therefore also my "son" (following the Mekranoti kinship system, the children of my "brothers" were my children, too, the children of my "sisters" being my "nephews" and "nieces"), and his constant companion, Kranjabjê. Both were senior bachelors and seemed pleased that I wanted to join them. Although we didn't go as far as the day before, they still managed to shoot a monkey. Back at the campsite, they joked about the noise I made while walking, imitating my clumsy way of stepping on branches and —with a plopping noise they made with their cheeks—the sound of my wet shoes. I felt moderately embarrassed, but enjoyed the mimicry and laughed along with everyone else.

I went on my third hunting trip the next morning, this time with my "brother" Kamkra. In spite of his age—he was about 45—he moved as quickly in the forest as the others. The advantage of going with senior men was that they stopped occasionally, listening to the different sounds and explaining what they were. I enjoyed these lessons immensely. When we'd been walking for about an hour, Kamkra suddenly froze and signaled me to do the same. He listened, sniffed, peered into the forest, and motioned to me to breathe more softly. "Niangdjy," he finally whispered. He'd spotted a deer. "You'd better return to the camp, because you won't be able to keep up with me from here," he said and vanished into the forest.

Turning back, I saw no path, no trail—nothing. So like a good boy scout, I tried to find my footprints. I was glad it had rained the previous night so that I could see them. Slowly but surely, I made my way until, after half an hour or so, I reached the spot where Kamkra had indicated that he'd dug up an armadillo the day before. Since he'd shown me that spot no more than 10 minutes before he'd left me, I could see how slowly I'd progressed on my own. I walked and walked until I could no longer find any footprints. I decided to search for the broken twigs the Indians leave as signs to indicate their way. Yet such twigs seemed to be all over the place. I realized I was lost.

It's hard to describe how I felt. It seemed best to stay where I was; surely the Indians would start looking for me. Having sat by myself for more than three hours, smoking one cigarette after another—at least the smoke kept the sweat bees and mosquitoes away—and listening to the birds and animals, I began to panic. Standing up, I tried to orient myself by looking at the sun. Since I knew that in the morning, we'd taken off to the north of the camp-

Hàkte, who found me when I was lost in the forest.

site, all I had to do was move due south. Or at least, so I thought.

I proceeded even more slowly than before, stopping frequently to listen, hoping to hear sounds from the campsite or one of the hunters on his way back to the camp. Once, standing motionless listening for any sound that might betray a human presence, I saw a black jaguar cross what might've been described as the path in front of me. There I was, totally unarmed, no more than 30 meters from one of the world's most feared felines. The jaguar didn't seem to notice me, however, and soon vanished. Hadn't it caught my scent? Hadn't it been hungry? Rooted to the spot, I couldn't have cared less. The important thing was that I hadn't been eaten. I waited for about 10 minutes and then started walking again.

About 20 minutes later, I heard a hunter singing way, way back in the forest. I yelled, but nothing happened. I was angry that I couldn't yell in falsetto

74

as the Indians did and started running toward the spot where I'd heard the singing. It began again, closer this time, so I stopped again and yelled "It's Jôkàr! Come here!" No response. Or so I thought. A few minutes later, old Hàkte appeared, carrying a pig on his back. I was exhilarated to see him; he looked surprised to see me all alone. When I tried to explain what had happened, he laughed and said, "So you lost your way? Here's the path, or didn't you see it? Let's go." As we walked, he muttered cheerfully that westerners really had "no eye." When the Mekranoti say that someone has a "strong eye" for hunting, they mean that he's good at it. Enemies or animals that are easily caught or killed are described as having a "bad eye"—or, worse still, "no sight." Having allowed myself to get lost, I wasn't in great company.

When we arrived back at the camp, there was Kamkra. His wife was already preparing part of the deer he'd caught. "So there you are," he said. "I was going to look for you after I finished eating." Since Hàkte and I had entered the campsite from the south, I realized that I must have made a circle around the camp. The Indians knew it too, and that evening there was much laughter at my expense. They asked me to describe everything I'd done in the forest, so I mimed the way I'd looked for footprints, the way I'd looked for broken twigs, the fear I'd felt when I saw the jaguar. Then I imitated the way I'd yelled at Hàkte. My audience collapsed with laughter, and I was thrilled, thrilled to be back among my friends.

The next day, Obet, the second village chief and probably the best hunter in the group, gently informed me that it might be better if I stayed at the camp, where I could "learn the old people's names"—in other words, continue my genealogical research. He added that the women would be glad to help me with that, and that the men trusted me to stay behind with them. I was grateful for his tact and appreciative of their trust. On the other hand, I was embarrassed that I was perceived as a handicap on hunting trips. As things turned out, I did occasionally join the hunters, but I was content to have the freedom to pursue my research without having to prove my hunting "skills."

Working on the Indians' genealogy, I soon ascertained that the village numbered 254 Indians. Trying to establish their interrelationships wasn't at all easy, however. For example, a woman considered her sister's children to be her children as well. Furthermore, the Mekranoti had no real genealogical depth, frequently not remembering the names of their grandparents unless they'd actually known them. Since according to their kinship system, affiliation was based on residential groups rather than on blood ties, they didn't need to know who their grandparents were. Still, after working for months on the subject, I was able to assemble files on over five thousand Mekranoti Indians, all of whom had lived in this century.

The day after my fiasco in the forest, we arrived at the Xixê River, at the exact site of the small garden Mel had shown me from the air. The Mekranoti had several clusters of gardens scattered all over the jungle. This insured a limited quantity of fruits and sweet potatoes during long forest treks. It was good to get to the Xixê. If you've never wandered in dense forest, it's impossible to describe the pleasure of being able to see a long distance. In the jungle, you can see as far as 30 meters at the most, so I could understand why the senior Mekranoti spoke with nostalgia about the open grasslands they'd occupied in the past. Everyone was pleased to have reached the Xixê, since fish were abundant there. Seeing how much the Indians enjoyed the change in diet, I asked why the Mekranoti hadn't located their village near a major waterway. Apparently, FUNAI officials had encouraged them to do

Concluding a forest trek, the women enter the village first, carrying their household utensils and smallest children.

75

this, because it would have made it easier and cheaper to reach the village by boat. The Mekranoti had refused—remembering the late 1950s and early 1960s, when so many Indians had died following initial contacts with whites—and had withdrawn to the forest. It was also the case that while the Indians appreciated major rivers as sources of fish, they hated having to cross them, since they didn't know how to make canoes. Since rivers were the most important means of communication in the Amazon rain forest, living along a major watercourse encouraged communication between communities. Living along smaller creeks, as the Mekranoti did, fostered isolation.

It's become fashionable among an ever-increasing number of anthropologists and biologists to emphasize the advantages of settling along major rivers, where the land is better for agriculture and where game is more abundant than in interfluvial areas. Living in an interfluvial area, the Mekranoti have fewer sources of animal protein than they would if they lived along a major river, but they've nonetheless managed to maintain a population that is large by Amazon standards. Their solution has

been to move their village every year or two and to go on regular long treks.

Having gathered over three hundred forest tortoises, we were nearing the end of our trek. We spent two days along the Xixê River, eating as much fish as we could and enjoying the scenery as well as the clean water. Then we returned directly to the village, a trip that took only three days. During our migration, we'd made a big circle to the south-east of the village, with the Xixê forming the north-ern- and northeasternmost sites we visited. The women and children arrived in the village first, while the men stayed near a small creek to paint themselves and rest before entering in appropriate ritual style. Singing as they approached the village, the line of men was led by Amjôkra, Krujêt's oldest son. Then came a group of young boys and a few other bachelors bringing rolls of dried palm leaves. They were followed by the married men, most of whom carried "ladders" of forest tortoises. The senior men came at the end. It was an impressive scene. One of the young leaders separated from the group and said a few words. Then the men scattered, some going into the men's house, others

76

joining their wives. Most of them went to the houses of the sponsors of the ceremony to place the "ladders" in front of them to be stored inside.

About half an hour later, as I was preparing for a bath in the river, I heard sounds of activity from the plaza. To my surprise, I found the men getting ready for a dance. Gathered in the men's house, they were painting their bodies black all over, wrapping their wrists with long strips of bark, and gluing white down feathers onto their hair. I was told that they were going to dance for the jaguar Kàjkwa had killed. Socializing the part of the rain forest they walk through in order to hunt, fish, cultivate, and so on is an important aspect of Mekranoti ritual life. This socialization process takes place in several ways. Place names are assigned to parts of the known forest. Different intrusions into nature are accompanied by ritual performances. For example, the cultivation of new fields is preceded by a dance whose structure closely resembles war ritual—hence it is a symbolic war. The singing of the men returning from the hunt is for the spirits of the animals they've killed, to compel them to stay behind in the forest. Each type of game has a specific song, which always begins with the cry of the dead animal. The performance of rituals is a language in itself. In Mekranoti society, rituals constitute the fundamental, summary expression of concepts and basic truths for the group. They also reflect the image the group has of itself and of the universe. Each ritual narrates a part of the cosmological vision and its mythological foundations, and establishes a link between humanity and nature, with particular emphasis on the relation between humans and animals.

Kàjkwa made a tour of the village, stopping in front of each house to address the inhabitants by saying "Aunt. Grandmother. I have killed the enemy. You can relax now. Ask your children to adorn themselves for the forthcoming dance." Shortly after he finished his tour, the men started dancing in two parallel lines, each man bent forward slightly with his left arm in front of his forehead, imitating the pose adopted when wailing at the death of a relative or meeting someone again after a long separation. They sang in falsetto, and some men carrying their rifles shot them into the air before joining the dance. The structure of the ritual of the slain jaguar strongly resembled that of

warriors returning from a raiding party which I'd managed to analyze through descriptions given by village elders. This came as no surprise, because the jaguar was considered to be the Mekranoti's worst animal enemy, and the attack on a feline was thought of as a symbolic war.

That afternoon, the men danced in the plaza for the *tàkàk* naming ceremony, each one holding a palm stick about three meters long. They'd removed the black paint, which had merely been applied with charcoal, from their bodies and wore different sets of ornaments. It was difficult for me to distinguish between the different dances, because the two rituals—the naming ceremony and the jaguar ceremony—were being held simultaneously. Ritual activities followed one after the other, and I had little time to cook, eat, or take a bath without missing something.

Later that evening, a singing session was held for the slain jaguar. Printi, my "brother-in-law," began by yelling absurd comments and imitating non-Kaiapo speech. The women, seated in front of their houses, all laughed a lot, and it was easy to see why Printi, renowned as a particularly good humorist, had been selected to perform this part of the ritual. Later, the men sang in low, serene tones just as they'd done in the forest, in order to remind the boys and younger men of songs that were only sung infrequently.

Early the next morning, the final jaguar dance was performed. This time, the ritual's warlike character was obvious. The men danced agitatedly, holding weapons in their right hands and stamping their feet. Following the dance, the arms of the young boys were scraped with a scarificator consisting of a triangular piece of gourd with sharp fish teeth inserted on one side. The scraping was done quickly. The incisions were deep enough to be painful and bled profusely. The boys weren't supposed to show pain or to withdraw their arms. Those who did were gently ridiculed by the onlookers.

I saw such scraping on several ritual and secular occasions. Children were scarified in extreme cases of disobedience or when they transgressed acceptable limits of behavior by, for example, killing a good hunting dog. Youths considered to be too lazy by the village elders were also scraped—in such cases, the incisions were limited to their thighs, "to make them run faster." Once I saw the arms of an adolescent boy scraped for forcing a young girl into sexual intercourse. In that instance, the boy's father invited the scraper to use the most "painful" of his scarificators. Fine permanent black tattoos on warriors' chests were made by rubbing charcoal mixed with medicinal herbs believed to strengthen or stimulate bravery into incisions made by scraping. Although the Mekranoti hadn't participated in wars since the early 1970s, most of the men had such tattoos.

All activities now seemed to focus on the *tàkàk* naming ceremony, which took on an additional dimension with the initiation of a few of the boys. Initiation can occur during early puberty, but isn't mandatory. Just as some children aren't ever honored at naming ceremonies, only about a fourth of all boys are initiated in the appropriate manner. Initiation is too limited a term for this particular event, because it started off with a ritual marriage. The mothers of several girls went publicly to fetch the boys of their choice. Since such ritual marriages are arranged between the parents of both parties, I was intrigued to see that in one case a woman without a daughter nonetheless picked out one of the boys. It was explained that her future daughter would become the boy's wife. Given how much younger these girls were than the boys, it was perhaps understandable that many of the boys courted other older girls, frequently marrying them. Although this was possible, the arranged marriages were considered to be better. In essence, however, the ritual marriages indicated young men's marriageability rather than establishing a firm bond.

The bachelors seemed to expend much of their energy on courting. Whether by actively and enthusiastically participating in communal activities such as dances or the hunt, or by paying particular attention to their apparel, impressing the opposite sex was their constant occupation. However, they also often charmed married women, who occasionally had bachelors as lovers. In fact, most bachelors were initiated sexually by married women. Although monogamy was the rule, adultery was quite common. The husbands clearly knew there was always a possibility that their spouses would have affairs with handsome bachelors—after all, they'd been bachelors themselves!—and that's why the most possessive of them tried to leave their wives alone as little

The final dance of the *tàkàk* naming ceremony.

During the *tàkàk* naming
ceremony, a man personifying
a jaguar ritually attacks the
honored children and their
guardians.

as possible. Since married men often tried to
seduce young girls, tensions between the two
groups of men occasionally arose. Generally speaking, people just "turned their heads," as they told
me, as long as those involved weren't too blatant.
Being caught in the act was considered a major
offense, however. The reaction of a cuckolded husband depended entirely on his mood, whom he'd
caught with his wife, and whether he'd suspected
the affair or not. Kôngri, the man I'd nicknamed
the Giant, left one morning on a hunt, but returned
almost immediately because he'd lost his balance on
a slippery path and ended up catching his foot on a
branch with thorns over four centimeters long.
Limping into his house, he found my "brother"
Kamkra making love to his wife. Kôngri made a
terrible scene, and Kamkra was afraid that he'd
start a fight. Unexpectedly, Kôngri announced that
in retaliation he'd sleep with Kamkra's wife, which
he eventually did. It turned out later that Kôngri
had been interested in Kamkra's wife for quite
some time, so he welcomed this opportunity to act
without risk to himself.

Things weren't always resolved so peacefully,
however. When Bepte one morning caught his wife
with his brother, he grabbed his club and chal-
lenged his brother to a club fight. "Hitting
together," as the Mekranoti call it, is a kind of
formal, stylized combat between two men or
between the members of two men's societies.
Armed with heavy spatulate clubs weighing over
five kilos each, the combatants take turns striking
each other at a point between shoulder and elbow,
until one of them is unable to continue or someone
intervenes to stop the fight. In this case, all of the
men gathered in the plaza, one group defending
Bepte, the other his brother. Feelings ran high until
Beprôrôk gave a long speech and succeeded in
cooling the agitated men down. Diplomatic as
usual, the chief combined mythology, history, and
his detailed knowledge of the men's family situation
and aspirations, finally proposing the perfect solution: the men would switch wives, just as so-and-so
had done in earlier times. This was done, and both
couples seemed particularly pleased with the swap.

Bachelors who courted unmarried girls didn't
have much to fear, unless the girls' mothers caught
them in the act, or they'd caused girls to lose their
virginity before they were considered old enough to
do so. Such cases were extremely rare. Since I had
several unmarried "sisters," I was often approached
by bachelors who wanted to set up assignations. In
the beginning, I refused to transmit such messages,
because I didn't want to get involved. One day one
of my "sisters" complained. Apparently, she was
upset because she'd missed an opportunity I'd
failed to inform her about with one of her friends.
She immediately asked me to transmit a message to
the same boy saying that she'd be waiting for him
that night. I was intrigued to discover that it was
often the girls who took the initiative. Bachelors
occasionally made clandestine appointments in the
bushes behind girls' houses. Since the bachelors all
slept together in the men's house, their pals knew
when one of them left and invariably tried to find
out whom he was courting. On returning to the
men's house, the bachelor in question was often
teased by the others, who'd say they recognized the
smell of his girlfriend or who'd tease him by saying
that his girlfriend had a giant vagina because she'd
already slept with everybody else. Although everyone knew this wasn't true, the constant joking about

romance seemed to enhance the close bonds between friends of the same age.

During the next two days, one ritual activity followed another. The young initiates spent most of their time outside the village, at a campsite not to be visited by women. A few senior men lectured the youngsters, teaching them traditional lore and specific songs. Each day, in the late afternoon, the initiates would make their entrance into the village, fully adorned with belts, necklaces, and ritual stone axes representing the bigger axes the men had traditionally used to lay out gardens. The wearing of the ritual axe indicated that these youngsters would soon have to lay out gardens for their wives. Each boy was invariably accompanied by a ritual friend, an adult man who acted as his tutor. After standing in the plaza for a few minutes, the boys would go to the houses of their "mothers-in-law," sit for a few minutes on their future spouses' beds, remove their ornaments, and then sneak to their own mothers' houses.

Four days after our return to the village, the women started preparing big earth ovens, so I realized that this was the final day of the ceremony. One by one, the tortoises' meat was removed. While the women did the butchering and prepared the festive meal, I entered the houses to watch the dancers being decorated. Unfortunately, the men didn't wear elaborate decorations this time. Their bodies were only smeared lightly with red annatto dye, and each man put on a small feather headdress, a necklace, and a back feather pendant. Those who were ready for the dancing gathered at the small campsite of the initiates. By the late afternoon, all of the men were there, as were the women and children who'd come to watch the scene. Women were allowed to enter the men's house only on such specific ritual occasions. People started insisting that I participate, by dancing for Mengrà, Kamkra's newborn son, who was therefore also my son. When I was told that the dancing would insure that all the newborn children became strong and healthy, I gave in, saying that I'd need to take time out to take notes and photographs. My body was quickly painted red all over, and Kôkôket, Kamkra's wife, fetched a feather headdress for me to wear. She also brought an extra-long palm pole for me to use.

Late that afternoon, the men all went to the landing strip and rehearsed briefly. Forming one big

Irepin, who was ritually "married" to me during my initiation — she never knew about it though.

circle, they all held long poles. Moving counter-clockwise, they sang while vigorously stamping their right feet on the ground. In the plaza, the all-night dance began after a brief speech by Beprôrôk. The women and children gathered to watch. The gleam of the fires made the dancers look like shadows emerging from the emptiness. During the first hour or so, the configuration of the dancers changed frequently. Groups were continuously formed and reformed, each group representing all the "fathers" of a newborn child. Since both biological and "classificatory" fathers participated in these groups, I had to dance in several such blocks. Those men who didn't belong to the category of fathers of newborn children danced at the rear. We stopped briefly every 15 minutes or so, when a man personifying a jaguar symbolically attacked the children being honored, who stood behind us with their ritual friends. We also briefly stopped at about 2:00 a.m. to eat the meals the women had prepared earlier.

The longer we danced, the more the men tired and the less dynamic the singing and dancing became. Whenever the "jaguar" thought the men hadn't sung hard enough or danced well enough, he remained seated on his mat, forcing them to start singing and dancing all over again, this time with more energy. At about 4:00 a.m., the dancing stopped once again. By that time, more than half of the men had withdrawn under one or another pretext. This was considered quite inappropriate, and so the remaining men discussed how to change their outfits to show that they'd continued to dance. It was decided that they'd each have a diagonal charcoal line drawn on their foreheads. This interruption lasted no more than five minutes. As if by magic, all of the dancers were reunited just as the sun came up, the shirkers joining in again so their women wouldn't know they'd been "weak." However, the diagonal charcoal marks served to distinguish the two groups, and the quitters were ridiculed by the women.

After the jaguar's final "attack," we performed a last round, singing and dancing with all of our strength and ending the dance by leaning our long poles against the walls of the honored children's houses. A few senior women and men related to them repeated the names that had been confirmed during the ritual. The *tàkàk* naming ceremony had come to its end. Exhausted, I joined a few of the bachelors for a refreshing bath. On our return, I noticed that all of the men had gathered in the men's house for a body painting session. The more I learned about this ceremony, the more I saw parallels with the one performed at the birth of a child that I'd seen earlier. In both cases, long reddened palm poles were carried by the protagonists. In both cases, too, the symbolic values of colors determined the sequence of application of body paintings. I inquired about the symbolism of the colors and learned that white, which was applied only in rare ritual decorations, was associated with the pure, "terminal" state of complete transcendence of normal society. It was, for example, the color of ghosts, and sick people who refrained from painting

Initiates being painted by their guardians during the last day of the long initiation ritual.

themselves were said to have "white" (i.e. un-painted) skin. Red, on the other hand, connoted energy, health, vitality, and "quickness" and was applied to foster growth and strength. Black was associated with transitions between clearly defined states or categories, with "borderline" conditions or regions where normal, clear-cut structures of ideas and rules of behavior were "blacked out;" black was therefore the color of normality, reflecting full participation in social life. The presence of the reddened poles and the light red body painting of the men marked a period of severe restriction, including respecting rigorous food taboos. All of these were like a series of protective measures enacted for the well-being of the newborn children. In fact, the dance of the *tàkàk* naming ceremony was often referred to as a "precaution for all children."

In the men's house after the all-night dance, all the male dancers had their bodies painted black with genipap dye. Those men whose children had begun to walk had only the sides of their bodies painted black; vertical white lines were made within the black zones by removing the fresh paint with the fingernails or with a special wooden painting comb. This design, called "striped body," indicated that, once the painting had disappeared, these men could once again be painted together with the other members of their men's society, something they weren't allowed to do for a year or so following the birth of their children.

A few hours later, I was amazed to hear that several men had gone into the jungle to hunt. Apparently, they weren't as tired as I was. The only thing I longed for was a good rest. Climbing into my hammock, I tried to sleep. But groups of children kept coming by to ask for things, or adults came and urged me to stay awake "as any strong man would." So I gave up and went visiting. Later that afternoon, I inquired about the initiates, whom I hadn't seen all day. I was told that they were at their campsite, of course. I was angry with myself, because I knew that an initiation of this kind took place only once every 10 years or so, and I was managing to miss part of it. While the naming ceremony had been completed, the initiation was still in full swing. I ran over to the campsite and saw the young initiates, their ritual companions, and a few elderly men sitting there listening to my old "uncle" Roiti. I remained with the initiates

almost constantly for the next four days, wanting to see each part of the initiation process, hear every speech, and help with the making of ornaments in their honor. I even slept in the small hut with them. We all had a wonderful time. The speeches and explanations were taken quite seriously, but we also laughed a lot. However, the more time I spent in the initiation camp, the more I felt that the adult men somehow felt uneasy with my continuous presence. Having decided to return to the village, I was told why my presence upset them. Married men were allowed to come and go as they pleased, but not youngsters or bachelors, unless they had a specific role like the initiates. Discussing my status as a bachelor, they finally came up with a perfect solution—at least in their eyes. I was to be initiated, too. They quickly decided which girl should be assigned to me: Irepin, a mere six year-old. "So," they announced, "consider it done. You now have a wife."

On the last day of the initiation ritual, all of the boys received special black paintings on their faces consisting of broad lines paralleled by two finer lines, with the space in between filled with red dye. Old Wajanga and my "brother" Kamkra applied the painting to the boys and to me. We then processed into the village. Nobody said a word. Taking our place in the plaza, we stood motionless in front of the men's house. One by one, adult men came out of the house, took us by the hand, and invited us to sit next to them. Beprôrôk then took us one by one to a corner of the men's house, where he hit our chests and backs several times against a wooden pole. This beating was meant to give us a magical infusion of strength and well-being, symbolically neutralizing the weakness and vulnerability of our infancy, for hardwood trees are potent sources of strength, endurance, and health in Mekranoti ritual symbolism. The initiation was over.

Nojabjê, the fierce warrior, seated with his youngest daughter
in the men's house. Having once worn a lip disk, he had
removed it a few years earlier.

In the 1970s, the men still use traditional weapons such as bows and arrows, especially during long forest treks. Although they prefer long wooden clubs as weapons, they frequently hunt with bows and arrows. Young boys are often trained in this skill. By the age of 10 or so, boys manage to gather enough fish and meat to be partially self-sustaining, only needing manioc flour or sweet potatoes from their mothers to complete their diet.

In the final phase of any major naming ceremony, the Indians leave on a long forest trek in order to gather a sufficient amount of tortoise meat to be distributed during the final dances. A maximum of fifteen live tortoises can be transported on a single "ladder," which might be three meters in length and weigh up to sixty kilos. Moving these towers through the forest is no easy task. Each day, the younger men leave before the others to clear a path through the undergrowth. Since two to three hundred tortoises are usually required for a major ceremony, the hunting operation may take a month or more.

Two young leaders, Bepkô and Ngrati, sitting in a forest camp during the trek on the occasion of the *tàkàk* naming ceremony.

Returning from a forest trek, the women carry all of the household utensils while the men carry the meat they've gathered. When adolescent girls reach marriageable age, they receive a special series of red marks on their chests and upper arms. The dots are marked with a burning stick, with small circular slices of rubber glued onto the wounds. These rubber patches are painted red during the first few weeks. Although they come off later, the marks remain visible throughout a woman's life.

Regardless of whether a warrior has killed an enemy, he receives tattoos on his chest for having participated in a war party. Each tattoo consists of a series of short parallel lines, running from near the shoulder down to the stomach alongside the navel. A specialist uses a scarificator to make the incisions and then rubs charcoal into the wounds to create permanent, fine black lines. Since men's bodies are always painted, it's rare to actually see these tattoo marks. I was able to photograph Padjê's tattoo because he'd remained unpainted for three weeks due to an illness in his family.

Opening a beehive in a tree to collect honey as well as beeswax to be used to manufacture headpieces for festivals.

During the last day of the
tàkàk naming ceremony, large
amounts of food are prepared. Since no food is wasted
in Mekranoti society, the shells
of the forest tortoise are filled
with manioc flour and put on
the hot stones along with the
meat and flour wrapped in
leaves, thus facilitating the
removal of the last bits of
meat from the shells.

During the final all-night dance of the *tàkàk* naming ceremony, all of the men dance with large poles. Initiates dance with ritual stone axes and also wear feathered necklaces, which they then may wear on other ritual occasions as a sign that they've been properly initiated.

In the final phase of the *tàkàk* naming ceremony, those children whose names are to be confirmed stand in the plaza with their ritual friends. Since naming is thought to be an extremely perilous occasion, several ritual friends—guardians who assist others during ritually important stages in their lives—are asked to stand next to the children being honored. All participants are adorned with parrot body feathers glued to their bodies and armlets with macaw tail feathers. Throughout the night, a man personifying a jaguar symbolically attacks the children and their guardians.

Tàkàkngre, the oldest son of my "brother" Ireteti, is one of the honored children during the *tàkàk* naming ceremony. For this occasion, he wore a special kind of ear plug with large mussel shells. From then on, he is allowed to wear these plugs on any ritual occasion, as a token of the fact that his great names had been ritually confirmed.

page 98
The ritual of the long "red leg" burity palm pole is one of a series of protective measures performed for the well-being of a newborn child and generally referred to as "precautions for the child." This ritual is performed a week or so after a woman has borne her first child. All of the young men and boys who call the new father Brother—and who therefore will refer to the newborn as their son or daughter—gather in the plaza to publicly declare their bond with the baby. This event marks the couple's transition from adolescence to parenthood and is the moment when a man joins one of the men's societies. The ritual lasts two or three days, and each day a different body painting is applied.

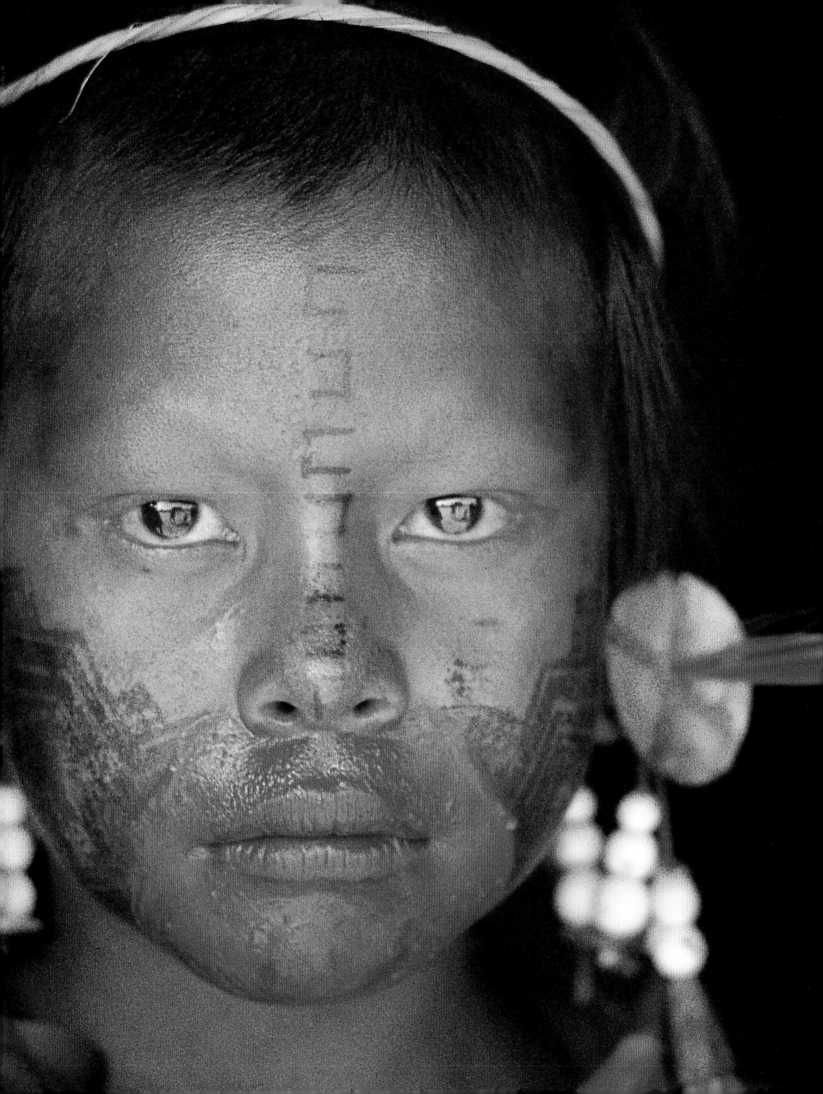

Complications in a Time of Relaxation

Nokàti cleaning in front of her house while stones are heated to prepare an earth oven.

Normal daily routine took over once again. The women went to the gardens in the morning, gathered at the bathing place by noon to chat, and spent the afternoon preparing food, painting their children, spinning cotton, and talking. The men hunted, made artifacts, met in the men's house, and discussed village politics. I made it a point to participate in many of these activities—even going on the occasional hunt—but life seemed monotonous now that the rituals were over.

I spent more and more time along the river. The most important of several bathing places was located to the west of the settlement. This was one of the most popular playgrounds for the children, the place where drinking water was collected, and the site of most of the Indians' daily baths. The river had an important social function for the Mekranoti. Deprived of an institutionalized meeting place like the men's house, the women usually met at the bathing place. At certain times, 20 or more women could be found there eating sweet potatoes, gossiping, commenting on village activities as well as domestic affairs, and sometimes discussing village politics. I spent a lot of time there playing with the children and, of course, eavesdropping on the women's discussions. I noticed that whenever the women stayed too long at the river, a few of the men would leave the men's house singing in order to let the women know they were coming. The women would then hastily pack up their things and leave the bathing place.

During the weeks that followed the *tàkàk* naming ceremony, I worked as much as I could with informants. Thanks to Kenti, my language skills were improving fast. As I began to study the group's history, I found it to be far more complicated than I'd thought, with more schisms and fusions, wars and migrations than that of any other Kaiapo group. I set up a fairly rigid schedule, working with two or three informants each day, spending about an hour with each because otherwise they'd become distracted. Kenti initially wanted to work with me in the morning. After a few days, he insisted on receiving a large payment for our sessions, because, as he put it, he'd "engaged" one of the bachelors to hunt for his family. I then proposed that he come in the afternoons, a suggestion he rejected by means of a series of silly arguments. It soon transpired that Kenti used the excuse of having to work with me in the morning to set up assignations with married women, knowing that their husbands would be away hunting. One day, things got out of hand. Kenti had given a flashlight he'd received from me to one of his lovers, and the husband suspected what had happened. An argument followed in the men's house, and that night Kenti came stealthily to my house, begging me to tell his girlfriend's husband that I'd given her the flashlight myself in exchange for some food. I told Kenti I didn't want to get involved. When he told me that Nojabjê—one of the group's most fearsome warriors—was the cuckolded husband, I finally agreed to back him up. I don't think Nojabjê believed me, but that was the end of the story, since he didn't have a leg to stand on. From then on, Kenti started working with me in the afternoons. Having refrained from amorous adventures for a few days, he soon started up again. Perhaps because I'd backed him up against Nojabjê, he discussed his escapades with me in detail, shedding light on aspects of village life about which I otherwise would have known nothing. The fact that Kenti worked with me in the afternoons turned out to be a fortunate thing, since it enabled me to work with the senior men in the mornings. They didn't seem to go hunting as frequently as the younger men and therefore had more time to spend with me. In the afternoons, I'd run over my notes with Kenti, having him translate the things I hadn't understood.

The more I worked on the group's history, the more I became aware of the many raids the Mekranoti had made during the last three generations. Although I hadn't planned it, I therefore found myself studying warfare. It finally became clear to me why the Brazilians living in the interior considered the Kaiapo to be one of the most warlike of Brazilian Indian tribes. Probably the most striking of all Kaiapo ornaments is the wooden lip disk. A few days after birth, a boy has his lower lip pierced. First a cotton thread is introduced into the hole, which will later be replaced by a wooden pin about the size of a match. When the boy is introduced into the men's house, the wooden pin is replaced by the first, small, round wooden plug. Gradually, plugs (and later disks) of larger diameter are used. By the time the man marries, the lip disk may already measure some 10 cm in diameter. Disks

were usually not enlarged in any significant way after marriage. Only four Mekranoti men still wear a lip disk. Most contemporary senior men had a lip disk at the time peaceful contact was made with the national society, but have either simply removed it — leaving, as such, a considerable and cumbersome hole in their lower lip — or had their lip surgically operated so that only a vertical scar remains as a witness of their once stretched lower lip.

The symbolic meaning of the lip disk can be compared with that of stretched earlobes: while the latter symbolically stand for a "second auditory canal" which has to promote "hearing" (=learning and knowing), the lip disk emphasizes speech and, more specifically, the power of oratory. Oratory is the most important means of persuasion for leaders and other (senior) men and leads to increased status in the community. Since only men are orators, and they are that from the time they have several

Ipebô carrying her baby towards the river for a daily bath.

The diameter of the light-wooden lip disks could easily reach twelve or more centimeters. Since the Mekranoti established prolonged contacts with the Brazilians in the early sixties, many men took out this lip ornament and boys no longer had one.

children, the stretching of the underlips is only begun when the youth is introduced into men's house. The insertion of ear-plugs and lip disks consequently responds to an ideological operation which has to stimulate hearing (and thus learning/knowing) and speach (oratory). The lip disk is therefore a symbol of male assertiveness and belligerence; values that were traditionally fostered in Mekranoti society. The senior men were proud of their warring past, since it was proof of their strength, bravery, bellicosity, and imperviousness to pain, all highly praised male virtues. The fact that I was a patient listener seemed to help elicit tales. After a few months, the younger men reacted negatively, however. Concerned as they were to live on peaceful terms with the Brazilians, they didn't appreciate my "asking questions about ancient raids" all the time. Young men considered warfare a thing of the past and regarded it as the immediate cause of the numerous pre-contact village disputes, the numerous killings in that period, and the splitting of the once huge Kaiapo villages into several smaller communities. Furthermore, they didn't want me to have the impression that the Mekranoti, in pre-contact times, "only made war." After a discussion on the subject in the men's house, the older men gradually began to avoid further conversations with me on the topic of warfare. I thus switched my focus to ceremonial life and name transmission.

After working for months on the latter topic, I was able to decipher the intricate naming system. As I worked, I noticed that people often pointed out where a name was "located" in the village. My research indicated that names as well as ritual privileges were associated with, and even "owned" by, certain households. The transmission of names and privileges, which was extremely complicated, was kept track of by the women, who saw that they were properly transmitted. Once I figured this out, I checked with certain people to see if they'd already transmitted their name to the appropriate person. I felt I'd made an important step in understanding Mekranoti society, and that years of teaching, hardship in the field, loneliness, boredom, and hours of asking foolish questions had finally borne fruit.

In the beginning, people would invariably interrupt my working sessions, but gradually they stopped doing so. As long as I kept the door of my house closed, they knew I was working. Interestingly, it wasn't I who told people to stay away, but the informants themselves, who made speeches in the village and in the men's house telling the others to stay away so that we could work in peace. I later realized that they did this in order to be able to talk more freely; whenever an unexpected visitor did come, my informants stopped answering my questions. Things weren't always easy, though. Some informants stuck to the point, while others digressed. One of the latter, wishing to provide as much detail as possible, took more than 15 minutes to tell me how his uncle had searched for hours for his pipe during a certain forest trek. I also worked with some of the women, who often brought their children along, providing yet another distraction. I was constantly reminded that anthropology is indeed the science of patience.

Having acquired a sufficiently sound linguistic basis, gathering information became a nearly full-time occupation. In addition to my work with informants, I often asked random questions to verify the information I received. Questioning the bachelors or young married men was often viewed as inappropriate. The senior men frequently would intervene with the observation that the men I was asking were too young to know anything at all. It soon became clear to me that many of the younger men, including Kenti, knew a lot about the topics I was interested in, but they never discussed them in the open, leaving this privilege to the senior men. So I checked much of my information with younger men and women in the rare moments I spent alone with them.

In studying the group's history, I discovered that in former times, the Mekranoti occasionally had sent young men to live with neighboring groups to learn their language and customs. When they returned home, these men passed along what they'd learned. In this way, the Mekranoti found out how to cultivate certain crops and had even adopted songs and ceremonies from their neighbors. Once I knew this, I finally was able to explain my own presence among them. I was there to learn as much as I could in order to transmit this knowledge to "my people."

With my mind entirely focused on my work, I hadn't really noticed that the rains had stopped. The dry season had begun, making life more pleasant. This time of year was characterized by hot, windy days, cool nights, and the almost total absence of mosquitoes. In addition, it was much less humid, and I felt physically able to do more. The season was known as "when it is good" or "the good times" by the Mekranoti. I now could walk around in shorts and sandals, without fear of being swamped by insects. One of my "sisters" (Nokàti or Nokàjabjê) or Kôkôket, my "sister-in-law," saw to it that I was painted at all times.

The men started laying out new gardens. For days in a row, they refrained from hunting, spending most of their time in the forest cutting trees. The Mekranoti were very demanding when choosing possible fertile oases; the ideal spot was a strip of forest where the overgrowth was not too dense, at the foot of some hills, not far from a river. They distinguished between different sorts of land and forest. The choice of a suitable place for a new village or field was not made lightly. Specialists in the group examined the soil, its color, and its composition carefully. Existing vegetation was also taken into consideration.

Once the laborious job of felling the trees had been finished, I decided to climb a mountain to the east of the village from which I imagined I'd have a nice view of it. I went there with two youngsters who acted as guides. It was a terrible climb, the last 50 meters or so being particularly steep, and I had to pull myself up by grabbing onto bushes and

Women bringing loads of palm leaves to roof a new house.

reeds. The view was indeed spectacular, but the hilltop was infested with ants and mosquitoes, so we didn't stay long. Returning to the village, we saw a pillar of black smoke, and my two guides panicked and started running. I followed close behind them. Approaching the settlement, we saw that several houses on the northern side were on fire. Some men entered the burning houses to save their belongings, which they threw into the plaza. After a while, I inquired about old Pykatyk, whom I didn't see. One of the oldest women in the village, she'd been sick for quite some time. Ireti, one of the senior bachelors and grandson of the lady in question, ran into one of the houses and a few seconds later emerged carrying Pykatyk, who was yelling that she wanted to remain in her house. I thought she'd

A newly constructed roof seen from below. Whenever they build a new house, the Mekranoti spend much time and energy on the roof. Their houses are especially solid and able to resist the harsh tropical climate for about 10 years.

gone mad, but when she died a few weeks later I understood that she no longer wanted to live. During the last days of her life, the weakened woman refused to eat and drink. She considered herself to be a burden to her small family and preferred to join her favorite daughter, who'd died two years before.

Kenti transcribing a Mekranoti myth in my house.

The fire had been started by a boy who'd been playing with some gasoline his father kept in a small plastic container. Due to the heavy winds, it soon spread, and 10 out of the 21 houses eventually burned down. Many precious trade goods such as rifles, ammunition, glass beads, pots, and machetes were lost. But the Indians were philosophical. Immediately erecting small shelters, they said that this was the perfect time to rebuild the entire village; they'd been talking about doing so, but kept putting it off. The rebuilding of the village soon occupied the entire community, taking several weeks during which people also did other things —working on their gardens, going on forest treks that had been planned. My house was also rebuilt. Still located behind Beprôrôk's, my new dwelling was much bigger and more luxurious than my old one. I was pleased that I had a house of my own, not only because of its size and comfortableness, but because I felt at home there.

"Accidents never come in ones" goes the expression. This was certainly the case in Mekranoti. People had barely gotten over the fire when a flu epidemic struck the community. In no time, almost everybody was sick. I understood how a simple flu or cold could wipe out an entire Indian village in no time. Since the sick Mekranoti were unable to work, not enough food was available, and this weakened the people even more. I saw strong men shrink to skeletons in a matter of days. Maria, a nurse, and Carlos, an agent, both from FUNAI, and I spent all our time and energy in health care. We cooked large amounts of porridge and rice, mixing it with all of the food there was left. We went round the houses repeatedly, treating the sick.

Within a week, three adults and three children had died. A FUNAI plane came twice, bringing medicines and food supplies. The situation finally seemed to be under control. Maria continued doing her rounds, giving vitamins to the recuperating population. One afternoon, as she was crossing the plaza on her way to the FUNAI house, a bullet landed at her feet. Although she panicked, she continued walking. Once home, she cried for hours, unable to understand why someone had tried to shoot her. I tried to find out what had happened. It turned out that Tepket, brother of Nojabjê, had lost his newborn son during the epidemic and blamed Maria, who'd given the child an injection. I tried to explain to Tepket that the injection couldn't have killed his son, but he refused to believe me. I therefore advised Maria to radio for a plane and leave immediately, which she did.

Less than a month after the epidemic, Ngra came running into the village in the late afternoon, shouting. Soon the whole village was in commotion. Ngra was the only Mekranoti man who seemed to have difficulty orienting himself, often getting lost in the forest, so that other men had to go out and look for him at night. On this occasion, though, his failing had worked to someone else's advantage. While on his way home, disoriented as usual, he'd made a detour and come across Bepte lying on the forest floor. While digging for an armadillo, Bepte had been bitten by a Bushmaster, a spectacular and highly poisonous snake that had been hiding in the armadillo's hole. Ngreti, Ireteti, and Wakongre set out to find him.

Over an hour later, they returned. First we heard their singing—songs of the Bushmaster and

of the dead—and a few minutes later, they appeared carrying Bepte's body. Bepte was taken immediately to the FUNAI house for treatment. Carlos did his best, but it was obvious that Bepte had already lost an enormous amount of blood. Realizing this, all of the Indians started singing the song of the dead, one of the most beautiful things I'd ever heard. Unlike many Mekranoti songs, this one was slow and especially melodious. Carlos radioed for a FUNAI plane for the next morning, but as he discussed Bepte's condition with the doctor over the radio, we all understood that it would arrive too late. Bepte died a few hours later.

The funeral rites started almost immediately and lasted for about three hours. Bepte's body was moved to his mother's house, and all the men performed a dance in front of it, re-enacting parts of rituals in which Bepte either had been honored or had played an active part. Then his body was taken to the cemetery to be buried. The Mekranoti bury their dead in a specific place outside the

On the occasion of the captive girl's death, only her adoptive mother and uncle Kôngri were present at the cemetery.

104

village circle. A grave consists of a circular pit
into which the corpse is placed in a sitting position
facing east. Then the pit is closed, and all of the
deceased's personal possessions—his or her drinking shell, weapons, ornaments, and so on—are
placed on top of it, so that the spirit can take them
along to its new abode. In the first weeks after a
person passes away, relatives put a little food and
drink next to the grave each day, because spirits are
thought not to be able to find their way immediately to their own village. Since the Mekranoti fear
human spirits a lot, Bepte's family lit a big fire in
the house at night to scare them away. Whenever
someone suspected that a spirit might be present,
I was called in with the flash attachment to my
camera, whose white light was thought to scare
them. Everyone wailed while Bepte was being
buried. In their grief, some of his kinswomen took
a machete and started cutting their heads, seriously
injuring themselves before other women seized
the knives. Days and even weeks after the burial,
Bepte's relatives occasionally would start wailing
again, in tribute to his memory.

A few weeks after Bepte's death, a young girl
giving birth began to hemorrhage. Considering her
as "almost dead," the Indians didn't pay any attention to the young mother. I visited her several times,
giving her medicines, checking her constantly
declining blood pressure, and bathing her motionless body. This was all I could do. When I asked for
help, no-one responded; everyone stood around at a
safe distance, discussing my "courage." So I went
alone to cut fresh leaves for the girl to sleep on.
Disappointed with the villagers, I only later came
to perceive their acute aversion to blood. For the
Mekranoti, blood is a dangerous substance. When
handling it, precautions are necessary, and special
rules are followed by anyone who comes into close
contact with it. After preparing and distributing the
meat of a freshly slain animal, its blood is washed
from the person's body as soon as possible, as it's
thought to be dirty, anti-social, and dangerous—
indeed noxious when in contact with human skin.
A Mekranoti myth relates how a man went berserk
after having had the blood of a tapir spilled on his
skin. Running off into the forest, he was partially
transformed into a tapir and eventually healed with
medicinal herbs by a shaman.

The girl, a captive from another group, eventually died. Many of the villagers were in the forest
at the time, and the funeral occurred without much
ritual. A few days later, however, when all the

Nokàti has chewed some food which she is transmitting to her daughter Nojaka.

Nokàti picking cotton in a garden.

villagers had returned, the inadequate burial came up for discussion. Ngrati, one of the young leaders, was particularly upset and said it was a scandal that the girl hadn't received a proper burial. In a long speech, he said he felt sorry not only for her but also for her biological mother—wherever she was— who'd lost her child during a raid and who couldn't be present for the burial, adding quickly that this might have been just as well since the girl had had an inadequate funeral. The villagers were embarrassed, and her death was rarely talked about after that.

What with the fire, the flu epidemic, and the deaths, many of the Mekranoti decided to leave the village for a while, to wander in the forest free from the evil spirits that were said to haunt their settlement. The villagers broke up into four small groups. One group stayed behind; another headed east so that the men could hunt birds whose feathers would be used to manufacture colorful headdresses; and the two others moved east and west, settling near the Xixê and Pitiatiá rivers to fish and lay out gardens that could be used during forth-

coming forest migrations. At first, I remained in the village, continuing to work with Krujêt and Beprôrôk. After a while, life got so tedious that I decided to join the group living along the Xixê, not only because I'd been there before and very much enjoyed the place but also because old Wajanga and my "uncles" Roiti and Tàkàkmê were there, and I wanted to work with them.

I went to the Xixê with Amjôkra, who'd become my assistant, cooking and washing up for me although I'd never asked him to do so. Since the FUNAI agents had such assistants, I suppose the Indians thought I needed one, too. Amjôkra proved to be discreet and extremely helpful, informing me of anything that was about to happen in the village and passing along any gossip. In exchange for his services, I not only gave him trade goods but also often helped him improve the basic reading and writing skills he'd acquired from Jean. I also became pretty close friends with Tàkàkpin, like Amjôkra one of the oldest bachelors in the group. Both were respected for "following traditional custom" in not marrying too young. Many men married around

106

much colder country if I had to sleep wrapped up like a package; they slept naked by a fire (although the truth was that they too preferred a good blanket). I took no food, no tape recorder, no cameras, no extra shoes. Traveling light, we were able to move quickly. The forest was quite dry now. I didn't slip all the time, and crossing log bridges was much easier. We arrived at the Xixê early on the second day. The camp looked quite different than it had a few months earlier. This time, no shelters were built; people slept on palm leaves and woven mats. Yet the ambiance was the same: relaxed, cozy, and friendly. We stayed for more than a month, and I had a wonderful time. Since everything happened in the open, I could freely discuss any topic with anybody.

Unfortunately, it soon became time to return to the village, where work continued on the new, bigger settlement and on the main gardens. First the cleared areas in the forest were set afire, so that the minerals in the dried trees would enrich the poor-quality earth. Right after the burning, the women sowed a wide variety of plants in concentric circles. There were many advantages to planting many different types of plants. For example, plants with big leaves shielded the soil against torrential rains and extreme drying, while tall plants provided protection against the scorching sun. Certain plants contributed to the fight against insects. Medicinal plants were usually planted on the boundaries of the field. Many of the latter produced nectar, which attracted a certain species of aggressive ants, the natural enemies of phytophagous, destructive insects. Although they may have appeared to be messy, Mekranoti gardens were extremely well structured. The fields were situated within a radius of four to six kilometers from the village and were managed by the women. Each family had its own areas in which it cultivated yams, corn, sugar cane, bananas and manioc. A few tropical fruits, cotton, and tobacco were also grown.

By September, everyone was reunited again in the main village. It was the tail end of the dry season, and the rivers definitely had reached their lowest level. The bathing place was unrecognizable. There was no longer any running water, merely a few stagnant pools in which people had to bathe and from which they took their drinking water. Many children and even some of the adults were

the age of 18, and such early marriages were regarded with a certain aversion by the senior men, who insisted that men should marry only when they'd acquired the essential knowledge and life experience to do so. The Mekranoti consider men who marry late to be strong and indifferent to pain, both highly appreciated male virtues, and to marry too soon is taken as a sign of weakness.

When we left for the Xixê, I hardly took anything with me: my hammock and mosquito net, a flashlight, a single pair of tennis shoes, an extra pair of shorts, T-shirts, and (one never knew) a shirt with long sleeves. I also took a heavy blanket, because the nights were extremely cold in the dry season. The Indians often teased me by saying that they couldn't understand how I could live in a

The men bringing baskets
filled with sand mixed with
small stones to create a surface
for the new airstrip.

struck by diarrhea or dysentery. At one point, the
situation got out of hand, and Alberto, the new
FUNAI agent, called in medical assistance, which
arrived the next day. In the second half of the
1970s, medical assistance was unquestionably
exemplary, the only problem being that sick people
flown into town for treatment often had to wait for
months before being flown back. The number of
FUNAI flights was severely restricted due to funding
shortages. Indians stranded in the towns sometimes
had disturbing experiences. The chief Obet, stuck
in Altamira with his son, encountered some Brazilians who showed him pornographic booklets that
horrified him. Since the people in the photographs
were white, he reckoned they were members of my
"tribe," so he asked me to explain them. I tried to
answer his questions, pointing out that normally
people in "my tribe" didn't have their pictures
taken while having intercourse. He nodded and
seemed relieved. Somewhat later, he observed that
perhaps the pictures had been taken "in whorehouses,
like the one I saw in Altamira." It made me mad to
think that someone had taken Obet to a brothel!

The result of Obet's unfortunate experience in
town was that he made several speeches insisting

that the Mekranoti women should wear underpants
at all times, or at least whenever strangers were
around. While clothing was being brought into the
village in ever-increasing amounts, soap often failed
to come, perhaps because it was so heavy to carry.
I could imagine the hygienic problems that might
develop if everyone wore panties or shorts without
being able to wash frequently. Fortunately, however,
the discussion tapered off, and after a few weeks
nobody spoke about the subject any more.

After the new gardens had been planted, the
men started laying out a new airstrip. For some
time already, FUNAI pilots had been complaining
that the six-hundred-meter-long airstrip was too
short for landing and taking off safely in their
medium-sized twin-engine aircraft. The Indians had
said that they were willing to build a longer, broader
airstrip provided that the air force, renowned in
Brazil for providing invaluable assistance to many
remote Indian villages, would extend their flights to
Mekranoti. The air force quickly agreed to do so. As
soon as the Indians had been informed of this, they
started working on their new airstrip, which was to
measure 1,250 meters in length and 25 meters in
width. The Indians worked hard, very hard, without

View of the Mekranoti village after it had been rebuilt in 1978, with a boy sitting in the big village square.

stopping. First they had to cut down some trees. As if they were laying out a garden, they burned the logs and branches. Then the ground had to be hardened. Particularly good sand with small stones in it was found about two kilometers from the site. Each day, the men carried hundreds of baskets loaded with sand to the strip, while others pounded the surface with large, heavy wooden blocks. The process of building the airstrip took months, and it took another year before the first plane was allowed to land on it. The ground had to be soaked with rain during the rainy season and then baked during the dry season. It was like a holiday when the first large air force plane landed, bringing tools and supplies to build a new, bigger FUNAI house with a nursery and pharmacy.

Unfortunately, it was also the last air force plane to arrive. When the Mekranoti discovered this, they were angry at once again having been deceived. Some of the senior tribesmen considered returning to the forest to take up traditional life again. "Why," they argued, "did we have to work like fools to get so little, when in former times we gathered more trade goods by stealing them from local Brazilians or by raiding other settlements?" I informed FUNAI of this situation, and a high-ranking agent promptly arrived to negotiate. He even spent a night in the village, something no official

had ever done before. Yet, instead of bringing good news, he merely urged the Indians to move to a major river. Most of the senior men abandoned the discussion when they heard this. The remaining men complained that their reserve hadn't been demarcated yet, but the official merely promised that he'd urge officials in Brasilia to get the situation sorted out as soon as possible. "In the meantime," he said, "this land is all yours, and if anyone trespasses, you can simply chase them away!" The Indians were all too happy to hear this, interpreting it as authorization to attack Brazilians in or near what they considered to be their traditional habitat.

A few weeks after the official's visit, the younger men were encouraged by their elders to show off their bravery and strength by attacking some skin gatherers who'd been reported in the far northeastern corner of their territory. Soon a war party had been assembled. Fortunately for the Brazilians, the Mekranoti scouts who'd been sent out to spy on them returned with the news that the invaders had already left. The raid was called off, but the young men remained agitated and anxious to show off their bravery to the elders. A few months later, the news arrived that military police had intervened in another Indian village when the inhabitants had attacked invaders. The Mekranoti realized that any attack they might undertake would inspire the same

109

reaction from the military, so the idea of a raid gradually faded. As a result of these events, the elders started talking about past conflicts again, thus helping me with my study of indigenous warfare.

In October, the time came for the Mekranoti to do their ritual fishing. While fishing was a year-round activity, big catches only occurred when the dry season was approaching its end and the water level was at its lowest. One morning, all the men went off into the forest to collect vines. I joined Ngreti who, as usual, took advantage of the occasion to teach me about plants and animals. Whenever he found the type of vine he was looking for, he'd shout "Whoo, whoo, whoo" and start pulling at it until he'd broken off a length. He'd then cut strips about a meter long and move on to look for another vine. As soon as one of the men had gathered the necessary number of vine lengths, he would carry the heavy bundle to a meeting point somewhere along the creek. While walking, he'd sing, just as if he'd killed an animal. The "whoo-ing" and singing were meant to enjoin the spirits of the vines not to be disturbed by the men's interference.

At the campsite, the senior men gave speeches exhorting the others not to be idle. When everyone had gathered, the men went into the water, which reached their waists. Then they began to strike the vines with small clubs. The sap released from the vines changed the oxygen content of the water, causing the fish to float to the surface because they couldn't breathe. A little way downstream, the boys—and later also the women and girls—gathered to collect the floating fish. Since the river was so small, the catch consisted only of small species. I also witnessed a similar fishing scene among the Kubenkrankênh, where the catch was much more impressive. For the Mekranoti, fishing wasn't as productive as hunting.

The ritual fishing was repeated several times, each time in another creek. The Mekranoti were well aware of the catastrophic consequences of this particular technique if it was practiced too often in one place. So as not to endanger the ecological balance by threatening the fish stock, they never performed the ritual twice in the same watercourse. They also knew that fish were only affected to a depth of about 80 centimeters, so they made certain to fish in water that was about a meter deep, so that some fish could escape.

Soon the rains were on their way again. The humidity increased at an appalling speed, and at times the sky was filled with threatening clouds. With the first rains came the first mosquitoes. I was soon forced to put on long-sleeved shirts and trousers again. The long and terribly exhausting but ritually more active rainy season was approaching.

Almost every morning the women left for the fields in the
early morning, carrying a burning wooden stick that
serves as a means to keep their pipes alight.

111

Kinjabjê, one of my youngest "sisters," lights her pipe with my matches. Spirits are believed to fear smoke, and so the women smoke almost constantly while working in the gardens. Scores of spirits are believed to haunt those places to find out how the women dig up sweet potatoes and manioc. The spirits also try to follow the women to the village. To deter them from doing so, the women spit in all directions and exhale extra smoke when leaving the gardens. This spitting and smoking thus has the same significance as the songs the men sing after successful hunts.

Digging for an armadillo, Bepte was bitten by a venomous snake and died within 24 hours. A few hours later all of the men and boys perform a dance during which they relive Bepte's ritual life.

The Mekranoti bury their dead in a specific place outside the village circle. Different personal possessions of the deceased are placed on top of it; the spirit will need them in his new home. For a time, food and water are placed near the grave in the hope that the spirit won't return to the village due to hunger or thirst.

The women go to the gardens almost every day to collect sweet potatoes, manioc, and bananas or other fruits, as well as tobacco and cotton. Leaving in the early morning, they return to the village with their heavy loads by noon. Although the gardens are laid out by the men, the women own them. Like the village itself, they are circular in plan. Circles are the Mekranoti's most potent symbol. The courses of the sun and moon, both thought of as mythological beings, are understood to be circular. A great number of ritual artifacts are circular, as are such objects of daily use as baskets, spindles, musical instruments, and ovens. Most dances and rituals are performed in circular configurations.

Of all people, the boys invariably were the ones most eager to leave on a forest trek. While on trek, they particularly enjoyed the additional freedom. They spent most of their time playing in the forest surrounding the camps.

Portrait of young Inhu wearing necklaces of
blue and white glass beads.

At the end of the dry season, when the river near Mekranoti dries up, holes sometimes have to be dug to obtain water for drinking and bathing. Many children often become sick, and occasionally a child will die. In traditional times, this rarely happened, since the Mekranoti wandered in the forest from one water source to another.

Fishing is a year-round activity; however fish are caught in large quantities especially when the dry season approaches and the water level is at its lowest. The Mekranoti use timbó lianes to do this. Men strike the liane sticks with small clubs for hours. The liquid released changes the oxygen content of the water. Because of the lack of oxygen, the fish then come up to the surface where they are easy to catch. Since the Mekranoti live along small rivers, the catch usually consists of small species of fish. In Mekranoti society, fishing is not as productive as hunting. Traditionally, all men should don a special feather headdress with feathers mounted in a framework of reed tubes covered with cotten string, as Padjê is proudly showing.

Traditionally, the Kaiapo, just like all Gê Indians, emphasise palm material in their ornaments, while the majority of Tupi Indians prefer feathers. When the Kaiapo had their first encounters with whites in the early nineteenth century, they fled to the west, penetrating an area predominantly inhabited by Tupi groups. The Tupi Indians were—and still are—experts in cotton work, making hammocks, finely woven belts, clothing, and other intricate weavings. Although the Kaiapo, like all Gê Indians, don't produce such items, their contacts with the Tupi led them to use cotton to manufacture their own ornaments, thus improving their own feather work and becoming among the most prominent feather workers of the Amazon. Today, cotton is still planted and spun by the women, but due to ever-increasing contacts with western visitors, the Mekranoti prefer red and blue cotton brought as gifts to anything they can make themselves.

Farewell
to my Friends

Each year, the rainy season seemed to be accompanied by some sort of plague. At first I thought this happened only in my imagination, until I heard that the Mekranoti had been hit by a serious malaria epidemic in 1968. Malaria isn't uncommon in the area, but it normally emerges as isolated cases. In 1968, however, it had reached epidemic proportions. Virtually the entire community had been paralyzed, and roughly fifteen percent of the population had died in the space of two months. Although the Mekranoti explained this calamity as being the result of witchcraft or the presence of a missionary, the malaria clearly had been brought by mosquitoes. My first rainy season in the field, the plague consisted of an invasion of mosquitoes of another kind. Nearly everyone resorted to wearing any kind of western dress they could lay their hands on. As soon as the number of mosquitoes diminished, the clothing was put away. The second annual plague I witnessed was of white scorpions measuring no more than three centimeters in length. Their size bore no relation to their dangerousness, however. The Mekranoti feared them more than big ones, though this may have been due to their color, white being associated with spirits. Some people were stung and suffered a lot of pain, but no-one died that year. Caution was the byword, however, because these scorpions seemed to like to hide in the boxes where I stored my food and clothes.

In another year, the area in and around the village was infested with tarantulas. These large, hairy spiders are rather sluggish, but can really bite. Although the poison isn't strong enough to kill, the area around a bite puffs up considerably, thus getting in the victim's way for a fortnight or so. The tarantulas also seemed to enjoy hiding in or around my boxes, and I even had one that settled in my primitive outhouse, thus making me hesitate to enter it in the evening or at night. One of my first encounters with a tarantula occurred when I was on my way to the river to bathe. I was sitting in the FUNAI house, leaning against the wall while I enjoyed a cigarette. Old Boti came in. When he saw me, he immediately said "Don't move!" Picking up a broom, he struck the wall with it just a few centimeters from my left ear. Looking over, I saw a tarantula squeezed between the wall and the broom handle. Although Boti laughed, I didn't seem to be able to. That year, there were so many tarantulas

Children play in the pouring rain. One girl carries a watermelon as if it were a baby.

that when I climbed into my hammock to read at night, I made a habit of placing a machete next to the kerosene lamp. Any time a tarantula came too close, I'd kill it with the machete.

The worst plague of all occurred the year the village was infested with cockroaches. Not big ones, but tiny ones. There were millions of them. At night, when I crossed the plaza, I could hear the sound of cockroaches being squashed with every step I took. Before sitting down, I'd lift the wooden block and drop it, and dozens of cockroaches would fall off. There were so many of them, and as there apparently wasn't enough for them to eat, they started attacking people. They bit anyone who slept without a mosquito net, and I'd occasionally hear children crying at night when they'd been attacked. The cockroaches became so ferocious that they even bore into people's ears, damaging those of two children. When the situation became really dangerous, it was decided to call in a particularly efficient service of the Ministry of Interior which specialized in such problems. When they came, everyone's belongings were piled in the plaza. After the houses had been sprayed, the Indians were urged to leave the area for a few days. Pleased with this suggestion, they all left immediately to spend a week in the forest. When they returned, only a few cockroaches remained.

I took advantage of the arrival of a FUNAI plane to leave the village for a short time myself in order to see a doctor about an infection in my ear. Collecting additional supplies and trade goods, I returned to the village about a month later. Things seemed to be going well in Mekranoti. When I arrived, my closest "relatives" wailed for me just as they'd have done for their real kin, with the women preceding the men. This ritual wailing wasn't an easy thing, at least not for me. The women cried in a high falsetto. Holding their right hands in front of their eyes, they recited everything that had taken place while I'd been away and said how much they'd missed me. In response, I was expected to perform the reciprocal male version, speaking as if I was being punched in the stomach, also holding my right hand up in front of my eyes. It was hard to listen while talking, especially as I was overcome by emotion. Tears rolled down my cheeks—I felt happy not only because I was among friends but also because their unexpected expression of affinity affected me deeply.

A new naming ceremony had started, the one of "the painted women." This was the sole ceremony in which women played the prominent role. Bepkô and Bonket, two of my youngest "brothers," were the sponsors. The mythological episode in which women became independent was remembered during this ceremony. This myth relates how men cheated on their women, who then left their village. The women painted their bodies to look like fishes and threw themselves into the water to live. The men soon were homesick for their spouses, and one enterprising man managed to catch his wife by attaching her favorite fruits to a fishing line. Body painting played a prominent role in this naming ceremony, which lasted for two months. The farther it proceeded, the more it made me reflect on the term used by the Indians for all of their major ceremonies. Strictly speaking, the phrase "the people who show off beautifully" is used only to refer to those being honored by a ritual. In some sense, though, I felt that this phrase was also meant to refer to the elegant manner in which children being honored (and the dancers accompanying them) were adorned. The term was therefore used most often in reference to naming ceremonies, because it was on those ritual occasions that the Mekranoti came closest to achieving their aesthetic ideal. The "beauty" of their shared efforts to socialize natural —and therefore dangerous—elements was also

Chief Beprôrôk (right) ritually wailing with a man who's just arrived on a visit from another Mekranoti village. Whenever the Mekranoti travel, they try to dress as much as possible like Brazilians.

124

important. However, the phrase could also be translated as "those who transfer beautifully." The act of transferal was also a characteristic of all the major

rituals, occasions during which series of ornaments whose wearing was considered to be a ritual privilege were not only worn but also transferred. The use of the great majority of these ornaments was restricted to those who'd inherited the specific right to wear them.

During these major ceremonies, I saw people performing ritual acts that also were thought of as inherited privileges. From an educational point of view, therefore, these ceremonies could be seen as "performed knowledge" in the sense that their enactment represented the accumulated learning of their performers over time. In any given ceremony, many people would be performing some participatory action either for the first time or for the first time on their own. This latter category of participants would have observed the action many times previously, of course. Such actions included particular, inherited ceremonial roles; the manufacturing of ritual paraphernalia; specific dancing and/or singing; and acting as ceremony leaders.

In essence, the ceremony of "the painted women" paralleled the *tàkàk* ceremony I'd seen before, except that more ornaments were worn and body painting was greatly emphasized. First there was the long training period, in which the shamans

125

introduced new songs. These were sung over and over again, until all the women and girls knew them perfectly. Then the whole village set out on a forest trek for a month to gather forest tortoises. On the villagers' return, a series of brief dances and singing sessions occurred one after the other, until finally, the women danced through an entire night. Most of these dancers wore large, impressive feather head-dresses. In addition, many had white down glued onto their hair, parrot feathers covering large parts of their bodies, and fragments of eggshell applied to their faces. It was as if many of the women had turned into "feathered people." This was both because all three components of the ritual costume consisted of materials obtained from birds and also because they more or less covered the dancers' entire bodies. These incomparably beautiful ritual costumes are the most sublime form of decoration among the Mekranoti.

The ritual participants lined up in two parallel rows and danced continuously in a big circle around the men's house. A few men—myself among them—were invited to participate by danc-ing for their nieces, while the other men took care of the children. My "aunt" Kôkôti took advantage of the situation to insist that I wear a penis sheath, which I reluctantly did. Though most Mekranoti men wore shorts, on some ritual occasions they still put on their penis sheaths, the bestowal of which —symbolizing biological maturity—traditionally occurred when boys had reached the age of about 15. I was pleased to see that the Mekranoti, in spite of my advanced age, had started to think of me as a full-fledged bachelor, but my enthusiasm dwindled as I discovered how incredibly uncomfortable it was to wear this tiny bit of traditional clothing. The sharp edges cut into my privates when I moved suddenly, so I tried to stay as still as possible until the sun set. I wore the sheath while dancing, know-ing that it was too dark for anyone to see my face occasionally contorted in pain. At about 3:00 a.m., after a brief meal, my sheath fell off, much to my relief. Since I couldn't leave my place without being questioned, I figured I'd pick it up during the next round of dancing. It was too dark for anyone to see that I'd lost it—or so I thought. I'd hardly moved a few paces when old Kôkôti, having noticed that I was "naked," started yelling. Soon everyone was awake, and general hilarity reigned. As we didn't

find the sheath, I was sure my leg was being pulled. Noticing that I was embarrassed, Beprôrôk took me to his house, where he quickly made me a new sheath. Completely "dressed" again, I regained my place among the dancers and continued as if noth-ing had happened, despite the laughter.

In the early morning, some of the men symbol-ically attacked a group of selected women. Armed

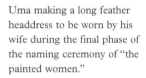

Uma making a long feather headdress to be worn by his wife during the final phase of the naming ceremony of "the painted women."

One of the honored children wearing all kinds of ornaments, among which are numerous strings of glass beads.

Two long lines of women and a few men perform the final dance of the naming ceremony of "the painted women."

with clubs, they each in turn ran toward a certain woman as if to abduct her. The women reacted fiercely, beating the men with their fists, pulling their hair, and resisting like mad. I felt sorry for some of the men who happened to be "abducting" a particularly resistant woman or one assisted by a group of kinswomen. I had the feeling that this ritual gave the women the occasion to act out any aggression they might feel. It was nonetheless a pleasant moment, accompanied by much gaiety.

Shortly after the ritual, Beprôrôk told me that my new name was Bepità. I felt particularly honored because this was the name of his father—my "grandfather"—and also because it was an important ritual *bep* name. My new name was soon adopted by everyone and relayed to other villages. That evening, Beprôrôk gave a speech in which he stated that he "had made me"—in other words, that I was his biological son. Two days later, my "brother" Ngreti was talking on the radio to the other Kaiapo villages and also spread the news of my adoption. Beprôrôk himself repeated it a few weeks later. As a result, whenever I arrived in another Kaiapo village, I was immediately told who my family was and never had any difficulty living and working among the Kaiapo Indians.

Although I felt honored at the time, I didn't fully understand the impact of Beprôrôk's gesture until later. Of course, not all members of my family took the matter as seriously as the others. But for those who did take it seriously, I was now a real kinsman. I was provided with adequate food. My "uncles" passed on to me the right to wear certain headdresses and to perform certain ritual acts. Members of my family also spoke more openly about matters I'd found difficult to discuss before. This final stage of adoption not only entailed a closer emotional tie with members of the Mekranoti community but also permitted me to see more clearly the relationships among relatives. There were a few constraints, though. If I wanted to spend time sitting with some of the women in front of their houses in the evenings, for instance, it would have provoked some irritation if I hadn't also done so with my "mother," "sisters," or "aunts." Sometimes my "sisters" went off to the fields together, dropping some of their children at my house "to keep an eye on them." I usually had a hard time controlling the gang and keeping them out of mischief.

When he adopted me, Beprôrôk was just over 70 years old and the eldest of all the Kaiapo chiefs. Each men's society has one or two active chiefs, each of whom has his own group of followers. The Mekranoti believe that a chief should know a specific form of ritualized oration, a series of recitative-like addresses that are seen as an integral part of several major ceremonies. A chief also should know "all about Mekranoti culture"—in other words, have a profound knowledge of and interest in that culture. A chief's knowledge is vast, comprising a familiarity with myths and tales, ceremonial lore, ritual speeches and songs, and a specific type of blessing song which only chiefs perform. Chiefs also have to "talk well," a reference to their eloquence as well as to the content of their speeches or the moral value of their suggestions.

The use of the term *chief* is in fact inaccurate for Mekranoti leaders, since they have no formal means of forcing their followers to obey them or to act according to their decisions. Mekranoti chiefs cannot command. If they try to impose their own desires on the community, they'll be abandoned or killed—as happened a few times earlier in this century. Chiefs therefore use oratory as their primary instrument of persuasion. During their speeches, they in fact articulate the consensus that is already growing within their men's society. Through orations—the articulation of moral values and the interests of their men's society—chiefs exercise their influence and prestige to get all of their followers to support their ideas. They also have to be bellicose in order to defend their group—acting as military leaders in times of war—and, above all, they must be generous. Generosity is thought of by the Mekranoti as one of the main characteristics of solidarity and is therefore one of the more important requirements for becoming a chief. To keep his followers united, a chief has to distribute the trade goods he acquires. Chiefs are therefore often the "poorest" members of the community. This is seen as an essential means of fostering the group's unity. Men who possess several of these characteristics may increase their influence within the community. And chiefs, who ideally personify them all, invariably figure among the most prestigious men in the group.

No formal rules exist for the succession of Mekranoti chiefs. The normal procedure for becoming a chief is a long one, beginning at early puberty, when several youngsters start training with senior chiefs. Such training takes many years. On becoming bachelors, one or two of the young men usually become leader of their age grade. This greatly depends on personal ambition—some men simply show no interest at all in becoming chiefs—as well as the support of comrades. After he has become a father, the young trainee joins one of the men's societies, and his training is stopped. On becoming a senior member of the community—by having at least four children or, even better, becoming a grandfather—the man who's developed himself as the most qualified and broadly supported of the leaders goes to the old chief who trained him to ask to become a real chief. If there are two existing chiefs in the community, the first one consults the other one. If the latter agrees, it is he who formally installs the chosen man by officially proclaiming his support.

Beprôrôk had been trained in his youth, but a few years before the time was right for him to become a chief, other candidates were selected. He therefore kept a low profile for many years, respecting his two contemporaries who'd been installed as chiefs. With the break-up of the big Mekranoti group into several villages in the fifties, however, Beprôrôk immediately became the chief of the biggest village. Now he was in the final stage of training four young man himself. Of these, his youngest son Bonket was most often mentioned as the successor to his father. Yet Bonket was greedy. He talked only of going to town to buy trade goods for himself and showed little or no interest in community activities. People started complaining about his attitude. One day, he simply walked out on his wife in order to marry a much younger girl. Although divorces did occur in Mekranoti, they always had to be approved by the council of elders. This time, however, the council didn't approve the divorce, since there was nothing to justify it. Stubborn as he was, Bonket left his wife anyway. That was the last straw. A few weeks later, Obet—the second village chief—approached Bonket in the men's house and, leaning on his club, began condemning Bonket's attitude. Although the men's house was full, no-one said a word. Bonket was visibly uncomfortable; he knew that he'd never become a chief. Such reproaches between chiefs and potential chiefs are called "to shout at"—I now knew why—and were extremely rare in Mekranoti society. I didn't see much of Bonket after his encounter with

Odet. Out of shame, he refrained from participating in communal activities and spent much of his time alone in the forest. When he entered the men's house, he'd sit alone in a corner, not joining in the conversation. A few weeks later, he took his belongings and simply moved to another Mekranoti village two hundred kilometers to the southeast.

Meanwhile, the status of my good friend Kenti was growing in the village. Kenti was an ambitious man. Being the sole Portuguese speaker in the community, he played a prominent role in the distribution of payments for the almost annual Brazil nut harvest. He also often traveled to town with the FUNAI agents to shop for the group. With Bonket out of the way, Kenti thought it was an appropriate moment to confirm his own position. Wanting to become a leader, he asked Beprôrôk to train him in traditional lore—the training given to adolescents in preparation for possible future leadership. The old chief refused, saying that Kenti, being a married man with children, was too old to be taught these skills. Kenti was disappointed. He told me that he'd expected this reaction, but had nonetheless hoped for some official recognition from Beprôrôk. When I asked Beprôrôk himself, he merely referred to the fact that Kenti was known as one of the village's most promiscuous men, a situation that already had led to denunciations and that had nearly developed into overt antagonism. Disappointed, Kenti also left the community and moved to Baú. He didn't stay there for long, however, for Obet pleaded with him to return. Kenti wasn't the same, however. He'd lost much of his cheerfulness and often failed to show up for appointments I'd set up to work with him. When he did, he often looked absent-minded and occasionally would complain about the lack of understanding in the community.

I'd already noticed stress in the village, but was as yet unable to grasp its meaning. The departure of Bonket and the incident with Kenti indicated that something was wrong. During our working sessions, Kenti also started talking more about the village's relationship with the Brazilians, describing events that had occurred during his visits to towns. He was particularly proud of one specific incident. When he'd been in Belém a few months before I'd arrived in the field, he'd received some money from Jean. Having decided to take a stroll in the suburbs, he went into a bar and asked for a soft drink. The customers in the bar saw that Kenti was an Indian and insisted that he drink the local rum, which he refused to do. When they began to pressure him, Kenti became furious and started smashing up a few stools and tables. By the time he left the bar, the other customers had been struck dumb. Kenti told this story with pride, both because it showed that he knew how to find his way around town and because he didn't drink alcohol in any form. While most Amazonian Indians use drugs or drink some form of alcohol, the Mekranoti traditionally are teetotalers, fearing and loathing anyone who drank—fearing the state of becoming "crazy," of losing control of themselves.

Life went on in the village. Things didn't improve much when the Brazil nut harvest came up for discussion. It was already quite late in the harvest when FUNAI contacted the Mekranoti, asking them to leave immediately for the Baú area. When it became evident that the Mekranoti were reluctant to go, FUNAI offered to send a plane so that one of the leaders could go and discuss the matter with people in Baú. Obet was the logical choice, since his father had been the main chief in that village. He returned with the news that people in Baú were already collecting nuts throughout the area and that they felt the Mekranoti should find other places to go to harvest. The reaction of the Mekranoti was quite fierce; they even considered taking up their old enmity against the people of Baú. I was amazed, knowing that many Mekranoti had relatives in the other group. As the discussion proceeded, the issues became clearer. Brazil nut trees grow very slowly, taking some 60 years before they reach the peak of their productivity. The Mekranoti, like all other Kaiapo groups, encourage the growth of various trees and bushes according to a complex system that involves planting species from far away closer to their own habitat. In the case of Brazil nut trees, they really do this for their grandchildren, not for themselves. Each of these planted trees has an owner, and the Baú people apparently had broken the rules by appropriating Brazil nut trees that had been planted by the Mekranoti in the remote past.

Sensing danger as radio messages were sent back and forth, the Baú people realized they'd get the worst of it if the Mekranoti attacked. The situation finally calmed down when the Baú people agreed to send part of the payment they were going to get for the harvest to the Mekranoti. The latter were pleased for several reasons. First of all, this meant that the Baú people in fact recognized that the trees in question belonged to the Mekranoti. Second, the Mekranoti were going to receive payment without having to work! Finally, the senior men had been complaining for some years that due to the harvest, the corn festival could never be performed. It was therefore decided that the festival would take place. Preparations began immediately, and since people talked about nothing else, it was easy for me to gather information. I was thrilled because the corn festival was the most important Mekranoti ceremony not related to naming.

The Mekranoti believe that an opossum taught them to eat corn long ago. Corn was essential in the rainy season. Planted in September–October, the first crops could be harvested in December–January. Ideally, the ritual was performed during the entire growth period of the crop. This time, however, the festival started in November. It lasted for more than four months and was without a doubt the most spectacular and enchanting ritual I saw while among the Indians.

Unlike naming ceremonies, which ended with a single all-night dance, the corn festival required no fewer than five such dances, two performed by young boys and three by adults. Three forest treks were necessary to gather the necessary food. Each time, another type of ornament provided the central theme of the dancing. In fact, the dances of the adult men were named after ornaments they wore: "the dance of the palm-leaf headband," "the dance of the beeswax hat," and "the dance with the ritual costume." Each dance was accompanied by different songs that were taught and practiced during the forest treks.

The farther the festival proceeded, the more I enjoyed it, because so many activities were planned. I had my camera in hand nearly 24 hours a day, trying to make sure I didn't miss a single phase. It was a very intense and incredibly profitable period for me. Just before we were to set off for our third and last forest trek, however, I sensed tension arising again in the community. It was decided that only the men would go on this trek, leaving the women and children in the village to obtain medical assistance—some of the children had intestinal problems. In the course of the discussion that fol-

lowed, debate apparently focused on which direction to take for the trek and how long it should last. The elders wanted to go east, which would take a longer time but would result in greater amounts of meat and palm straw. The younger men wanted to trek west, hoping to be away for a shorter period. Things were left unresolved. The more "traditional" group took off toward the east, while the others stayed behind in the village "to remain close to their spouses," a choice the elders viewed with contempt.

During that last trek, which in the end lasted a mere two weeks, a general feeling of depression seemed to have struck the men. Only 26 out of a total of 60 participated. Almost every night, conversation focused on the recent crisis. No one seemed enthusiastic about hunting or moving to the next campsite. I often heard the men say that there was "no longer . . . a good mutual understanding" within the village and that a split was about to occur. Ngrati, one of the young leaders, suggested that the bachelors and recently married men form one men's society, while the older men formed the second group. Such re-orderings of men's societies occurred frequently in Mekranoti history and often reflected attempts to reduce tension within the community. As he explained to me later, Ngrati wanted to unite both of the existing younger men's groups in the hope that this would stimulate them to come to the men's house more often instead of staying in the residential houses with the women. According to him, the younger men's lack of involvement in the men's house was the essence of the disagreement. Ngrati felt that such "asocial" behavior restricted male solidarity. Although the idea of rearranging the men's groups seemed to receive the approval of those who'd participated in the trek, things changed when we returned to the village. Several older men, among them Beprôrôk, resisted the idea by arguing that there were enough adult men to maintain the two numerically balanced men's societies and that they preferred things that way. The discussion then died.

In spite of the political commotion, the trek had been successful, since enough meat and palm straw had been gathered. For some reason I started to feel very weak. Was this my response to the general feeling of tension, or had I gotten dysentery? As soon as we returned to the village, I spoke to João, the new FUNAI nurse, who attributed my mal-

Kamamak has a beeswax hat glued onto his head.

aise to general exhaustion and gave me a vitamin injection. Two days later, the corn festival came to an end. The men spent the whole day preparing their outfits, turning the men's house into an ornament factory. All sorts of feathers were assembled and mounted on rigid hooflike supports mounted on wooden sticks. I now realized why so many birds had been caught during the last months and why the Mekranoti's pet parrots had been plucked so often. The Indians keep 35 species of birds as pets. Parrots and parakeets, eagles, toucans, and macaws constitute the most important species, their feathers being used in various ways to fashion ornaments. Once a bird has been shot down with a special blunt arrow, it's brought to the village, where it's kept in a cage. As soon as it has recovered, all of its tail and wing feathers are plucked so that it can't fly away. The bird is free to roam in or around the house, but as soon as new feathers grow, they're plucked again. The body feathers of some birds are also plucked on occasion. Those of parrots and parakeets are used for ritual costumes; those of macaws are used to make ornaments such as feathered hats; those of eagles are used to make pendants for big feather headdresses; and those of harpy eagles are used as hair coverings or to make

specific ornaments such as feathered hats or necklaces. In actual fact, such birds are less pets than feather factories.

The village was bursting with activity. While the women prepared the meat, the men spent their time either in the men's house or at home, where their spouses glued parrot body feathers onto their freshly painted bodies. People who specialized in applying eggshells visited each house to glue them to the men's faces. The dancers then went to the men's house, where beeswax was molded into hats directly on their shaved heads. Rigid feather headdresses mounted on sticks were inserted into the tops of the beeswax hats. As if this was not enough, most of the men donned additional long feather headdresses of yellow, green, or reddish feathers, as well as necklaces, belts, bracelets, and so on. By 5:00 p.m., they all were ready for the dance. They assembled in front of the men's house, where Beprôrôk gave a brief speech. Then the dancing began. The men formed two groups corresponding to the two men's societies. From each group, Beprôrôk selected one man who'd lead his group and who'd have to dance for the entire night. The leader of the first group ran forward, dancing and singing, turning when he'd reached the opposing

The men start one of the all-night dances of the corn festival.

group, which then followed him. Eventually, both groups mingled. After singing a verse, the two groups separated again, and the leader of the second group "fetched" the members of the first group. The fusion and separation continued all night. Whenever a group started moving, and as long as both groups were united, the men sang in a high falsetto. As darkness fell, the time during which the groups remained united was extended, with the men singing two or three verses before separating again.

As usual, I was invited to participate. I was painted and given a beeswax hat and rigid head-dress on a stick. The light green parrot feathers inserted into the latter represented one of the specific ritual privileges my "uncle" had transmitted to me after the final phase of my adoption. Although I stayed up the whole night, I withdrew from dancing occasionally because I felt so weak, but also because I loved watching the spectacle. The dance ended in the early morning. All of the decorations were removed and stored in boxes for the next celebration. I crawled into my hammock to rest. I was exhausted and felt terribly feeble. I hardly slept that day and the following night. In spite of the two blankets covering me, I felt cold all over and shiv-

ered most of the time. I realized that I'd been hit by something worse than dysentery. When I looked at myself in my dirty mirror, I noticed that my eyes were yellowish, and I knew that something was wrong.

I felt weaker with every passing minute. Taking a walking stick, I dragged myself across the village. People kept asking me what I was doing. All I could say was that I felt sick. I made my way to João, who took my temperature, looked into my eyes, and palpated my abdomen. Without saying much, he promptly settled me on the platform that served as a bed and set up an IV. drip. I soon fell into a deep sleep.

When I awoke again, it was quite late. João came right over. "I'm not going to hide anything from you," he said. "As far as I can tell, you have falciparum, the worst type of malaria." He hesitated. "The problem is that I don't have the specific treatment for that kind of malaria here. But that's not all. You know that malaria attacks the liver. Well, it seems to me that, in addition to malaria, you also have hepatitis, which similarly attacks the liver. You must have noticed that your liver is seriously swollen, haven't you?" I asked what he could do. "You know the radio hasn't been functioning for several weeks now" he replied. "There's not much I *can* do. I'll keep you on the IV., but the only real solution will be for a plane to show up. As far as I'm concerned, you have to get out of here as soon as possible!"

News of my illness soon got around. Many people came to visit me that day, and the next, and the one after that. Nokàti and Nokàjabjê, two of the "sisters" to whom I was closest, spent hours with me—at least while I was awake—just sitting there or talking about things people were doing. They told me that a new naming ceremony had started, once again the one of "the painted women." Tears rolled down my face when I realized I was stuck no more than two hundred meters from the village, where so many interesting things were taking place. Seeming to understand, Nokàti placed her hand on my arm, the tenderest gesture any Mekranoti had ever made to me.

I never knew whether Nokàti arranged it or not, but the next day, in the afternoon, the women performed their singing and dancing session on the plaza in front of the FUNAI house. Some men and women came and moved the platform I was lying on, IV. and all, toward the plaza, so that I could watch. Although I was shivering from yet another malaria attack and felt even weaker than before, I enjoyed seeing the women dancing in single file, singing in nagging tones, and accompanying themselves with gourd rattles. Shortly after the dance was over, I was moved back to my prison.

Two days later, João informed me that my situation wasn't improving and that he feared the worst. He said he'd try to get the radio to work the next day. That morning, he was already at it by 7:00 a.m. Around noon, he came running back, saying "It works! My God, what a miracle!" We finally were able to radio a message about my condition to the FUNAI office in town. Yet João's enthusiasm evaporated when he received their answer. The doctors insisted that I be moved immediately to a hospital, but the head FUNAI official wanted to know whether I had enough money to hire a plane. I didn't. They responded that they couldn't help me. João tried to mediate by mentioning the many months I'd spent alone in the village providing medical assistance, the time I'd helped FUNAI out on a mission that was meant to prevent a war between two Kaiapo villages, and so on. His

attempts failed. The next afternoon I felt so weak that I could no longer get up. Even calling for someone to help me became impossible. I knew something had to be done. I got someone to call João and wrote a note:

> Message from Gustaaf Verswijver to the Belgian Embassy in Brasilia, the Ministry of Interior, the President of FUNAI in Brasilia, and the Head of FUNAI in Belém. I have been struck down with malaria and hepatitis in the village of Mekranoti. Lack of financial means hinders me from hiring a plane to transport me to a hospital. I have been lying here for six days already. There are no adequate medicines available here. Thank you for your attention.

João felt that this message constituted an attack against his superiors—in a way it did—and preferred not to send it. When I asked him if he thought I could get out of the situation alive without additional help, he said no. Aware of the awkwardness of his situation, I took my message back and added at the bottom: "I've asked Mr. João to transmit this message. It is my sole and entire responsibility" and signed it. The message was transmitted that afternoon.

Early the next morning, a reply came from Belém. They were trying to get in touch with a pilot to transport me that same day to the hospital in Itaituba. João was amazed. I was told later that my message had caused a flurry of activity in the cities. At the Ministry of Interior, they had called FUNAI to ask what was going on. When my lack of funds was mentioned at the ministry, they replied, "Well then send an air force plane!" The president of FUNAI, himself an army general, called a general of the air force, who promptly said there'd be no problem. They'd either send a helicopter from the base at Cachimbo or another plane from Brasilia or Manaus. By that time, the Belgian Embassy had entered the game. They felt embarrassed that the air force had to intervene to save one of their citizens and suggested that FUNAI arrange to hire a private plane at the embassy's expense. The problem was that the embassy didn't have authorization to help Belgians in trouble. So the ambassador contacted the consul in São Paulo, whom I'd known well for years. Officially, he couldn't do anything either, but he agreed to approach some prosperous Belgian citizens who might sponsor such an intervention. This was what worked in the end.

That morning, the only private pilot from Itaituba who knew the location of the Mekranoti village was on a flight to a distant gold mine. His wife expected him back by noon. In fact, he got home much too late to insure a safe flight that day. Nonetheless, at the instigation of Roberto, the FUNAI official at Itaituba whom I'd known when he'd been an agent in Gorotíre, the pilot decided to risk it. Taking off at 4:00 p.m., he arrived at Mekranoti at 5:30. João and the Indians went to meet the plane, offering the pilot and his co-pilot shelter for the night. Declining the invitation, the pilots urged everyone to get me to the plane immediately. Since it was already getting dark, no-one had expected such a reaction. João came with a few men to the house, wrapped me in a dirty hammock, hung the hammock from a wooden pole, and carried me hastily to the plane, luckily remembering to grab my notes and technical equipment. Although I could barely see the Indians, I did hear several people crying. Among them I recognized Nokàti and Nhàkpu, another one of my "sisters." I was lifted onto the plane, and less than two minutes later we were off.

Once in the air, I felt secure, but not for long. Darkness fell, and neither of the pilots could find his way. I heard them saying that it was too late to reach Itaituba and that they'd aim for Alta Floresta, a fairly recent settlement on the other side of the important Cuiabá–Santarém road. That flight would take "only" an hour. The farther we flew, the more nervous the pilots became. Every few minutes, they each took a drink from a bottle of rum. When we finally reached Alta Floresta, the airstrip proved to be invisible. So the pilots radioed the airstrip and asked that lights be set out along both sides of it. That took at least 15 minutes, during which we circled the town. Finally, it became possible to see the landing strip. Taking another quick swig from their beloved bottle, the pilots brought the plane down. A jeep was waiting to take me to the hospital.

I must have fainted before arriving at the hospital, because I don't remember much about it. In fact, I don't remember much about Alta Floresta at all. At sunrise, we were off to Itaituba, where Roberto was waiting for me. Driving like a mad-man to the hospital there, he registered me as a FUNAI agent to facilitate things. Without delay, I was put into a room and taken care of. Blood samples were taken; nurses ran back and forth to get IV.'s and additional sheets. The man in the other bed didn't look well at all. When the doctor came in, I inquired about his illness. "It's malaria falciparum with hepatitis," the doctor replied. "He won't make it. But then what do you expect. He's had it for five days already!" When I told the doctor that I'd been ill for eight days, he refused to believe me, checking with João to confirm my story. That same afternoon, the man in the other bed died.

I stayed in the hospital for 10 days—paid for by FUNAI!—and then for a further 10 days at the FUNAI delegation. I then proceeded to São Paulo. The doctors advised me to leave the area as soon as possible and to travel by plane to avoid shocks. They also suggested that I stay in Europe for at least six months or a year; if I caught malaria again any sooner than that, it could be fatal. I traveled by FUNAI plane to Altamira where, by coincidence, I met my "brother-in-law" Obet and Ngrati, who were there making arrangements for the next year's Brazil nut harvest. When I left Altamira, they came to the airstrip to say good-bye. Standing there waiting as I checked in, Obet and I started crying in the traditional Mekranoti way. "Come back as soon as you can," he said. "We'll all be waiting for you. When you arrived, you were like a child. You couldn't speak or behave like a human being. Now you've learned a lot. You've become a full-fledged bachelor. It's time for you to marry. When you come back, we'll arrange a marriage for you. You're like one of us now." Five minutes later, I was sitting in a plane flying over Altamira. Below me, I could see Obet and Ngrati staring up at the plane. Although I sensed that this was more of a farewell than a good-bye, it was eight years before I saw my friends again.

This page and pages 136/137
In central Brazil, the year is divided into two seasons: the dry season ("winter") from May to October, and the rainy season ("summer") from November to April. The dry season, "when the weather is nice," offers an extreme contrast with the rainy season, which is characterized by torrential downpours, the overflowing of most streams and rivers, and the annoying presence of insects. The Indians refer to this period as "when it rains." Life continues in spite of such heavy precipitation, though wandering through the flooded forest is far from easy.

During the last few days of the annual "painted women" naming ceremony impressive dances are performed daily. During these dances, the women wear many ornaments whose use is restricted by inheritance. For example, in the early part of this century, a Mekranoti man stole a mirror during one of his raids on a Brazilian settlement. He made a sling attaching this mirror to the bottom. Since the other people in the village admired his ornament, he declared it to be his ritual privilege and transmitted the right to use mirrors in ornaments to his granddaughter. Even today, the man's descendants have the exclusive right to manufacture ornaments with mirrors. In the mid-nineteenth century, another man went to live for a time with the neighboring Karaja Indians. From them he learned to crochet wristlets, which craft he adopted and handed on as his ritual privilege.

During the naming ceremony of "the painted women," several children have their great names ritually confirmed. Approaching the final phase of the ceremony, the children are carried by ritual friends during the long dancing sessions. On those occasions, they often wear large feather headdresses and series of beaded ornaments such as necklaces and wristlets.

Pages 140/141
Near the end of "the painted women's" naming ceremony, the women jointly go into the forest almost every afternoon to collect palm leaves. Gathering behind the houses, they enter the village in single file. The leaves are displayed on the floor in the sponsors' house serving as mats for the women's singing sessions that evening.

138

Akamàn distributing gourd rattles to the women during one of the final dances of the naming ceremony of "the painted women." He'd received the ritual privilege to store and distribute these rattles.

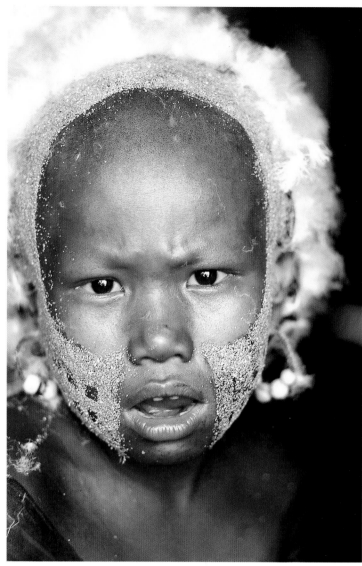

The white down feathers adorning the dancers' hair come mainly from vultures, herons, or harpy eagles. To apply them, the hair is first smeared with sticky latex. The creation of this decoration is connected with the mythological battle in which Kukrytwir and Kukrytkakô, two mythological heroes, killed a dreaded giant bird. Just as the heroes wore down feathers in their hair after this battle, present-day Mekranoti warriors decorate themselves in this way during the ritual performed after a clash with an enemy (human or feline) and during the ritual that precedes the laying out of new fields. In addition to the down feathers, crushed shells of tinamou eggs are glued to the warriors' faces and up toward the crowns of their heads, shaven in the *jôkàr* hairstyle. These same decorations are worn by women and girls during "the painted women's" naming ceremony.

During the final, all-night dance of the naming ceremony of "the painted women," the women and girls dance adorned with major feather headdresses. These headdresses are often stored in boxes or bags in the houses, and before being used, they're hung in the sun for a few hours. Major feather headdresses are made of the tail feathers of parrots, crested oropendolas, or macaws. One by one, the women perform brief dances in the plaza, showing off their headdresses and indicating that they're ready for the final event of the ceremony. Several myths and stories indicate a strong correlation between these headdresses and the sun and moon, whose rays the macaw feathers are thought to resemble. Whenever a lunar or solar eclipse occurs, all of the pubescent girls perform a dance wearing such major headdresses, preceded by the men, who shoot burning arrows into the sky.

The ceremony of "the painted women" has a male counterpart, during the initial phase of which the men perform a series of dances wearing smaller feather headdresses which, in mythology, are specifically related to the moon.

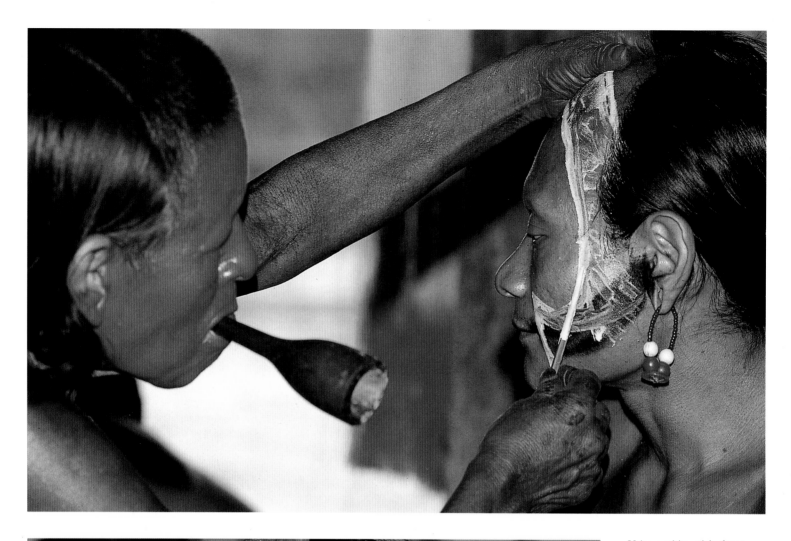

Using a white, sticky latex, blueish pulverized egg-shells are glued to Poti's face. Such decorations are only applied on those rare occasions when dancers literally have to "show off their beauty".

At the start of the final dance of the corn festival, two young men are selected to perform the ritual blessing every half an hour or so. These young men invariably are people who've been trained for years by a senior chief in order to become chiefs themselves, if they wish to. Both men stand outside the group of dancers, flanked by the few female participants who've been given the ritual privilege to accompany this spectacular event. While these women and girls are as beautifully adorned as the male dancers, they don't wear beeswax hats with feather headdresses, whose use is restricted to men. When the dance starts, some senior women perform ritual weeping in memory of dead kinsmen who took part in past performances.

The Mekranoti believe that once upon a time they inhabited a higher level (the sky), from which they descended to the present level (the earth). Some Mekranoti were left behind in the sky, and the fires they light at night to keep themselves warm can be seen from the earth: these are the stars. The Mekranoti also believe that the world isn't spherical, but rather consists of a rounded rectangular part representing the "end/tip of the sky" (the west) flanked by two rounded extensions (the "arms" [north and south]). These "arms" protrude onto a triangular extremity representing the "beginning/root of the sky" (the east). In the middle of all this is a circular "center" that represents the circular Mekranoti village, the center of the universe. This horizontal world-image is symbolically reproduced in the *kutop*, a Mekranoti decoration in the form of a beeswax hat. Feather headdresses—here, one is being made by Pakamrêk—are mounted on top of such beeswax hats and represent the sky. The stick symbolizes the rope by which the Indians descended to earth. The *kutop* is worn during the most important phases of the corn festival.

This page and pages 156/157
The final dance of the corn
festival is the most spectacular
scene I've ever witnessed. First
the men gather in front of the
men's house, and then they
start their all-night dance.
Nearly all of the participants
wear the ritual costume consisting of parrot body feathers
glued onto the body and tinamou eggshells glued onto the
face, in addition to different
types of feather headdresses.
Just as the Mekranoti shamans
are said to change themselves
into birds so that they can participate in the supernatural
world, non-shamans decorate
themselves in this "feathery"
way to effect a metamorphosis.
Ritual costumes are mostly
worn at the conclusions of
phases in which individuals
have undergone transforma-
tions. Wearing ritual costume
must therefore be seen as a
means of making the necessary
return to the community.